NAME ME, I'M YOURS!

BABY NAME BOOK

By Lydia and Joan Wilen
Illustrations by Greg Metcalf

FAWCETT COLUMBINE · NEW YORK

Published by Fawcett Columbine Books, a unit of CBS Publications, the Educational and Professional Publishing Division of CBS, Inc.

ISBN 0-449-90159-9

Printed in the United States of America

First Fawcett Columbine Edition: April 1982
10

Created and Designed by Mary Ellen Enterprises
Art Director: Tom Oberg

Contents

INTRODUCTION BY
Mary Ellen

I'm in the business of solving problems, and boy, oh boy did I have one a little over six years ago.

When I got pregnant, my husband Sherm and I began thinking of, among other things, a name for our upcoming blessed event. Foolishly, I thought naming a baby would be the easiest part of what was to come.

Well, one night Sherm and I got a pad and pencil and sat down and made two lists — my selections for girls and boys names, and Sherm made his own list. Wow! Sherm (I'm blaming most of this on his strange brand of creativity) came up with names I'd never heard of — (make that names no one had ever heard of). Some of the more normal gems from his boys' list: **Purvis, Haskell, Duke, Francis,** and **Marion.** And if a girl: **Cosette, Ingleberta,** or **Ponce.** At this point I have to admit not all of mine were terrific, (**Wellington, Winston, Napoleon**). After what seemed like endless arguments over selecting names, we settled on Andrew, which everyone seems to be happy with.

Now, six years after I needed them, I found two clever women, Lydia and Joany Wilen, who have compiled some fascinating information on the "Name Game." The Wilens can give you some very creative guidance for your first big decision as a parent.

Wish we'd known the Wilens back then. Have fun, learn what names mean, and **GOOD LUCK!**

Mary Ellen Pinkham

i

CHAPTER ONE

Names, American Style

Our long history of names began when the first settlers arrived in America with their Dutch, French and Spanish names. These names were soon altered, added to or replaced by English names. Later waves of immigrants brought even more variety to our names, with their colorful culture, in the 1800s. This process continues to this day.

In spite of the foreign influences, a great proportion of names in America are still very traditional. **John, William, James, Charles** and **George** for boys and **Mary, Ann, Elizabeth, Margaret** and **Catherine** for girls are still high on the roll call. This doesn't mean that all American parents are conservative when it comes to naming their children. American parents are certainly the most adventurous child-namers, accounting for names like **Starr, True, Moon Unit** and **China.**

Americans are also influenced by the media and many of the more popular names come from television, film and music. Witness the popularity of the name, **Michelle,** after the Beatles' song of the same name.

It's interesting to see the shifting popularity of names through the decades:

1830		1900	
John	Mary	John	Mary
William	Sarah	William	Ruth
James	Jane	Charles	Helen
George	Elizabeth	Robert	Margaret
Charles	Harriet	Joseph	Elizabeth
Henry	Martha	James	Dorothy
Thomas	Margaret	George	Catherine
Daniel	Catherine	Samuel	Mildred
Edward	Caroline	Thomas	Frances
Andrew	Eliza	Arthur	Alice

1950

Robert	Linda
Michael	Mary
James	Deborah
John	Patricia
David	Susan
William	Kathleen
Richard	Karen
Thomas	Barbara
Steven	Nancy
Gary	Carol

1970

Michael	Jennifer
David	Michelle
John	Amy
Jeffrey	Kimberly
Robert	Lisa
James	Julie
Christopher	Dawn
Mark	Kristin
Steven	Laura
Scott	Kelly

1975

Michael	Jennifer
Jason	Amy
Matthew	Sarah
Brian	Michelle
Christopher	Kimberly
David	Heather
John	Rebecca
James	Catherine
Jeffrey	Kelly
Daniel	Elizabeth
Steven	Julie
Eric	Lisa
Robert	Melissa
Scott	Angela
Andrew	Kristen
Mark	Carrie
Aaron	Stephanie
Benjamin	Jessica
Kevin	Christine
Sean	Erin

1980

Michael	Jennifer
Jason	Sarah
Christopher	Elizabeth
David	Jessica
Matthew	Amanda
Brian	Michelle
James	Melissa
Joseph	Angela
Eric	Nicole
John	Kristin
Steven	Christina
Robert	Kelly
Daniel	Rebecca
Ryan	Megan
Andrew	Heather
Jeffrey	Rachel
Nicholas	Katherine
Jonathan	Amy
Joshua	Laura
Justin	Stephanie

CHAPTER TWO

What's in a Name?

A Psychology of Names

Names influence us more than we might like to admit. Most of us would accept a blind date with **Debbie** or **David** over one with **Daphne** or **Delbert**.

Many of us have definite preferences toward certain names. For example, it seems that Johnny Carson has a leaning towards women whose name start with the same two letters of his own first name: **Jody** was his first wife, **Joanne** was his second, and his third wife is named **Joanna**. The first female guest on "The Tonight Show" when Johnny took over in October, 1962, was **Joan** Crawford. When Johnny is going to be away from the show, the woman he most frequently calls upon to substitute for him is **Joan** Rivers.

Psychologists claim that most of us have "name prejudice." Witness Napoleon. It is said that the French emperor grew shrewd and bold while defending his name against the taunts of classmates.

In an experiment involving 80 elementary school teachers, name prejudice was found to have an effect on grading. Each teacher was given eight compositions by fifth and sixth graders, all of comparable quality. Instead of the children's real names appearing on the compositions, four popular names— **Michael, David, Lisa** and **Karen**—and four unpopular names—**Elmer, Hubert, Adelle** and **Bertha**—were substituted. The results were shocking. Michael and David came out a full grade higher than Elmer and Hubert. Karen and Lisa did a grade-and-a-half better than Bertha. Apparently, Adelle was a more middle-of-the-road name and fared better than Bertha. In fact, one teacher gave Adelle the highest grade. She explained that she had always thought **Adelle** sounded like an intelligent name!

Another experiment involved a group of 10 and 12-year-olds. In this one, two psychologists set out to determine whether there was a correlation between a name and the popularity of the child. Again, the results were shocking. The children with popular names (James, Gary, Stephen, Peter, Mark, Diane, Linda, Carol, Barbara, Cindy and so on) were preferred, by far, as friends over children with unpopular names (Gardner, Stockton, Aubrey, Florian, Faber, Myra, Gillian, Simone, Meta, Rosemede and so on).

What's in a name? When it comes to people, it's better to go through life with your name working for you than against you. Keep that in mind when naming your baby.

CHAPTER THREE

Twenty Questions

Things to Consider

Selecting a name for your baby is one of the peerless privileges of parenthood. And a great responsibility, too, since the name you select will be the one you want your baby to carry throughout life.

Few parents are likely to be as casual as those who sent their daughter into the world as Miss Ima Hogg, or those who registered their twins as Bigamy and Larceny. Nevertheless, before you decide on a name, it is well to ask yourself these 20 questions.

1. Who's on First?

Your last name should be your first consideration when choosing a name.

If you have a short, common last name like Smith, Jones or Brown, don't be afraid to be daring. Select an interesting first name (*Ogden Nash, Jessamyn West*).

If your last name is long and complicated, keep the first and middle names simple to provide a nice contrast (*Mary Ellen Higginbotham, John James Audubon*).

You might even consider using a last name as a first name. Boys' names like Clifford, Russell, Stanley and Nelson, and girls' names like Kimberly, Stacey, Leslie and Kelly were all surnames that have become accepted first names.

The practice of using a family name as a first name has traditionally been used by the well-to-do to honor an illustrious forebear. But be careful! Some English names, such as Wellington, Brentwood or Throckmorton, may sound snobby or affected when used this way.

2. What's on Second?

Go ahead, give your child a middle name. There's no extra charge for it on the birth certificate.

A recent survey revealed that about 95 percent of American men and 92 percent of American women have a middle name. Another indication of their popularity is the initials "NMI" on automated lists. "NMI" stands for "No Middle Initial," which seems to be such a rarity these days that it rates a special designation.

The giving of middle names is a relatively recent custom. It didn't catch on in England until this century, even though it was a common tradition in Spain and Germany. Often among German immigrants, the mother's family name was adopted as the middle name. This custom seems to have taken root. Today, many parents choose the mother's maiden name for a girl's middle name.

If you're still not sold on giving your baby a middle name, think about this: Almost every President of the United States from Ulysses Simpson Grant to Ronald Wilson Reagan have middle names, and four-fifths of the people in Who's Who have middle names.

3. Is It Easy to Spell?

A name may look good on the printed page of a gothic novel and that may be the last time it's spelled correctly.

Give your child a name most people can spell right the first time they try.

It is annoying to have one's name misspelled most of the time.

Byron, the English poet, said, *"Thrice happy he whose name has been well spelt in the despatch."* In other words, your child will be a lot better off with a name that's easy to spell.

4. Is It Easy to Pronounce?

It's no fun going through life correcting people on the pronunciation of your name.

Comic columnist, Harry V. Wade, tells about a gentleman of importance in Egypt whose name is Aziz Ezzet. He says, *"His name can be pronounced by opening a soda bottle slowly."*

Do your child a favor and find a name that's easy to say.

5. Does Rhythm Count?

Choose a name that has a rhythmic sound when combined with a middle and last name.

The general rule: *an unequal number of syllables in any order.* In other words, if your last name has one syllable, find a first name with 2 or 3 syllables.

Listen to the rhythm of the following names:

Kris Kristofferson *(1 and 4)*   **Raquel Welch** *(2 and 1)*

Dorothy Parker *(3 and 2)*   **Dwight David Eisenhower** *(1, 2 and 4)*

Margaret Mead *(3 and 1)*   **Ralph Waldo Emerson** *(1, 2 and 3)*

Frank Sinatra *(1 and 3)*   **Rutherford Birchard Hayes** *(3, 2 and 1)*

With unequal numbers of syllables, the name seems to flow. That doesn't mean names with equal numbers of syllables will not sound good. The best way to know which names work is to say them aloud and try them out on other people.

7

6. Is It a Boy or a Girl?

Think twice, three times, maybe more before selecting a unisex name for your baby. We all know about, *"A Boy Named Sue,"* but do you really want to do that to your child?

On the other hand, there are many names that are appropriate for either a boy or a girl *(Corey, Fran, Lindsay, Merle, Terry or Tony to name a few)*.

If you've found a boy's name but you're blessed with a girl, feminize the name by adding a new ending:

ENDINGS	**EXAMPLES**
a	David/Davida, Leon/Leona
ia	Julius/Julia
een, ene	Paul/Pauleen, Martin/Martene
ina, ine	Joseph/Josephina, Josephine
ette	Paul/Paulette
elle	Daniel/Danielle
ice	Bernard/Bernice
issa	Mel/Melissa
inda	Mel/Melinda
lyn	Joe/Joelyn

7. Does It Sound Right?

A sound name is one that sounds good. The rhythm helps a lot but there are other considerations for smart-sounding names.

Stay away from names that have the same endings *(Norman Goodman, Phyllis Loomis, Martha Bertha Luther)*.

Alliteration is fine *(Farrah Fawcett, Marilyn Monroe, Ronald Reagan)*. Names that rhyme are not so fine. They're comical sounding *(Rita Sedita, Oona Goona, Ella Wella, Stewart Pruitt)*.

Avoid having the first name end with the same sound with which the last name begins *(Ralph Foster, Arnold Day, Jane Nesbitt, Michelle Lear)*. It's hard to tell where the first name ends and where the second one begins.

One more bit of sound advice: Listen to the way the names sound together —the first, middle and last names.

8. How About Junior?

Alexander, a soldier who fled from a skirmish, was later confronted by Alexander the Great. The fearless Macedonian king said to the cowardly soldier, *"Either change your name or live up to it!"*

Being a namesake can be tough on a youngster, especially if he's got big shoes to fill. It can also be confusing, especially later in life, when a call for "Bill" may bring both father and son to the phone. Giving your child his own individual name will help avoid these potential problems.

But, if it's a family tradition, go ahead; John Jay Smith III has a pretty impressive ring to it. Besides you'll be in good company. Many famous Americans are namesakes including astronaut **John Glenn, Jr.;** civil rights leader **Martin Luther King, Jr.;** author **Kurt Vonnegut, Jr.;** and actor **Douglas Fairbanks, Jr.** to name a few.

9. Is It Too Trendy?

Once upon a time, it was fashionable for parents to name their children after popular characters from romantic novels and history: **Clarissa, Guinevere, Catherine.**

During the 1960s, one-word, "meaningful" names were hip: **Chastity, Free, God.**

The style-setters today are television and films. Look what happened to the name **Jennifer**. It erupted into popularity because of the movie *Love Story* with its heroine of the same name. Jennifer has remained the most popular girl's name since 1970.

Oddly enough, trendy names seem to wear better on girls than they do on boys. You may occasionally hear of a Cary or a Kirk, but Elvis and Errol have never caught on.

If you choose a trendy name, you run the risk of dating your child. A name can actually pinpoint an era. Unless that's your aim, avoid a *"name of the hour."*

10. What's So Funny?

Have you ever been with a group of people who start reciting names of people they know—names that are funny—names you're relieved aren't yours? For example:

- Publicist **Spencer Hare** named his daughter **Hedda.**
- **Mr.** and **Mrs. Dwopp** named their little boy **Wayne.**
- A Parisian music teacher named her eight children, **Doh, Ray, Me, Fah, Sol, La, Ti** and **Octave.**
- **Mr.** and **Mrs. Cianci** *(pronounced See-Ann´-See)* named their daughter **Nancy Ann.**
- Football player, **Carl Eller**, named his daughter **Cinder**.
- There were identical twins **Kate** and **Duplicate.**
- **Mr.** and **Mrs. Pease** named their son **Warren.**
- **Beach** ... The children of this Florida family were named **Rocky, Coral, Sandy** and **Pebble.**
- **4 E Chittenden** was the name of an electrical contractor in Stanford, California.
- Speaking of numbers, **1069** was selected by **Michael Peter Dengler** of Minneapolis, Minnesota when he wished to change his name to a number. The court turned him down.
- **Never** ... was the first name of a builder in Tulsa, Oklahoma, whose last name was **Fail.**
- **Toot** ... was the name changed to by an Indian originally called **Shrieking Loud Train Whistle.**

It may be funny when you're talking about other people's names, but not when it comes to your child. Do not give a name that lends itself to teasing.

11. Why Not Something Unusual?

The parents of **Eartha Kitt** were farmers. After several bad harvests in a row their luck changed in the same year their baby girl was born. To mark the event, they called her **Eartha.**

Children with names like Houston, Dallas and Austin reflect their parents' pride in their native cities. While you may encounter a few Detroits, Jerseys or Peorias, there are more than a few Georgias, several Denvers, a couple of Tennessees *(Ernie Ford, Williams)*, and one well-known Cleveland *(Amory).*

It's fine to create a new name. But remember that it's your child that must bear it. The last thing you want to do is give a name that sounds odd or ridiculous.

Believe it or not, on the record are such names as **Erie Canal Johnson, Eiffel Tower Sutherland,** and **States Rights Jones,** not to mention children with names such as **Kiwanis, Payola, Faucet, Xylophone, Fairy** and **Vaseline.** But these seem almost normal when compared to **E. Pluribus Ewbanks** and **If-Christ-Had-Not-Died-For-Thee-Thou-Wouldst-Have-Been-Damned Barebones,** a name later shortened to just plain **Damned Barebones.**

While an unusual name may lend a certain distinction to your child, weigh your decision carefully.

12. What Does It Mean?

Historically names had meanings. Though we tend to pay more attention to the sound and harmony of the name, remember that your child may be embarrassed when (s)he discovers its meaning. After all, most names have been handed down thousands of times, and meanings change from generation to generation. Here's an example:

Waldo - German - **Ruler**
Waldo - English - **Mighty**

So, while the meaning of a name is a consideration, it's a minor one.

13. What's Your Initial Reaction?

There's a superstition among some cultures that if the initials of a child's full name spell a word, that child will be wealthy. Even if that's not the case, pay attention to the initials of the names you choose for your baby. If, for example, they just happen to spell something nice—**L.U.V., J.O.Y., S.U.N.**—that's a little bonus for your baby. Just beware of nasty, burdensome acronyms—**T.U.B., S.H.Y., Z.I.T.** It only takes a second, and your child will be grateful.

Another possibility is an acronymic-nickname—Thomas Oliver Moore (**T.O.M.**); Nancy Alberta Nye (**N.A.N.**).

14. How About Nicknames?

Nicknames are usually contractions of given names (**Robert:** *Robbie, Bobbie, Bob, Bert*); sometimes they're take-offs on surnames (**Smith:** *Smitty, Jones: Jonesy*); and, occasionally, they stem from physical characteristics (*Slim, Red, Speedy*).

It's better to give your child a name that lends itself to a nickname (*William, David, Theresa, Abigail*) than to give your child a nickname (*Bill, Dave, Terry, Abbie*). Think of the variety a child has to choose from if his name is William rather than Bill. You give your child a chance to grow with his name (from **Billy** to **Bill** to **Willie** to **William,** then **Grandpa Will**).

Nicknames are important to children. They seem to promote a readiness for

12

friendship and the idea of being *"one of the boys or girls."*

Lots of famous people have nicknames. In sports there's **Yogi, Casey** and **Bubba.** We all know **Groucho, Sissy, Johnny** and **Ed.** Crime is up to its brass knuckles in nicknames. Remember **Bugsy, Lucky, Legs, Pretty Boy** and **Baby Face?** Society pages are filled with 'em ... **Bobo, Bebe, Bitsy** and **Binky.** The White House has had its share from **Honest Abe** to **Ike, Jack, Jerry, Jimmy** and **Ronnie.** And, on a musical note, there's the **Count** and the **Duke.**

Irving Lazar, a prominent literary agent, made a bet with Humphrey Bogart that he could get him five movie contracts in five hours. By the end of that day, Bogie had five movie contracts and Mr. Lazar had the nickname, **Swifty.** To this day, he is known, internationally, as **Swifty Lazar.**

15. What About My Roots?

It's fine to go back to your roots or to combine roots in a name, but be careful not to do it at your child's expense.

Wouldn't you want to laugh if you were introduced to **Ming Chang Epstein, Plato Kowalski,** or **Hernando Jones?**

The general rule for avoiding conflicting ethnic or national names is to have the first name agree with the nationality of the last name.

16. Can I Put a Little "Dash" in It?

We've all seen the name **Olivia Newton-John.** Your child can also have a little "dash" in her name.

Nowadays, more and more women are using their maiden names along with their husbands' surnames, separating them with hyphens. These names are being passed on to their children.

In some cases, hyphenated names are long and awkward. Parents can encourage their child to shorten the name once (s)he's old enough to make that kind of choice. For example, **Robert Mark Gillespie-Martinson** can be changed to *Robert Mark Gillespie* or *Robert Mark Martinson*.

17. What's on Your Mind?

Names conjure up pictures. The pictures are based on our own personal experiences. Another consideration in choosing a name for your baby is the picture a name brings to mind.

Eleanor Links Hoover, writing in Human Behavior, was both amused and puzzled by the "instant identities" conveyed by stereotypes, that is the picture we imagine when hearing a name. Make a snap judgment and see whether you agree with Eleanor Hoover that . . .

Mary *is virtuous.*
Jane *is cute and dull.*
Kathy *is traditional.*
Cecil *is a sissy.*
Audrey *is formidable.*
Katie *is spirited.*
Debbie *is giddy.*
Jerry *is breezy.*
Muriel *is plodding.*
Tony *is passionate.*
John *is stolid.*
Buddy *and* **Wally** *are dumb.*

Martin *is nondescript.*
Harvey *is bumbling.*
Bart *and* **Mack** *are he-men.*
Jean *is straightforward.*
Jennifer *is interesting.*
Patti *and* **Jody** *are tomboys.*
Nina *is warm.*
Missy *is prissy.*
Rita *is lively.*
Bill *is dependable.*
Bruce *is stuffy.*
Hortense *is impossible.*

18. Can I Bring Religion into It?

Catholic children are required to have the name of a saint as the first or middle name. Jewish children are named for deceased relatives.

If your religious persuasion is a consideration, see your religious leader and learn all about the special guidelines and traditions associated with naming children.

19. Can I Personalize a Name?

Consider everything around you—the time of year the baby is due *(April, May, June, August)*; maybe the flower and birthstone of that month; consider the maternal and paternal family names; a name in a song both of you love *(See THEME SONGS)*; consider a character from your favorite work of literature *(Melanie, Ashley, Evangeline, Eustacia, Tess)*; an historic figure you respect and admire—everything that touches your personal life can suggest a name.

20. Is That All?

Last but not least, there's one more major consideration ... **your name**. *Do you like it? When someone says your name, are you happy to hear it? Would you like to change your name? Want a simpler one? Want one that's more intriguing?*

By now you should be getting the message. Put yourself in Baby's place and try to imagine if (s)he is going to be pleased with the name you've chosen, based on—what else?—your experience with **your name**.

CHAPTER FOUR

Names...Making Them Legal

Birth Certificates

Before your baby is born, you'll probably ask yourself one or more of the following questions:

- **Does the hospital take care of the birth certificate?**
- **What background information am I required to submit when my baby is born?**
- **What are my state's legal restrictions when it comes to a choice of names?**
- **How does a stepfather go about legalizing a name change for the baby? How do foster parents go about it?**
- **What do I do if I decide to change the baby's name after the birth certificate has been registered?**

BE PREPARED! Each state has its own legal requirements regarding the registration of a baby. Look in your telephone directory under *Birth Records, Vital Statistics Office,* or *Department of Health* and get all your questions answered **before** your baby arrives!

After your baby is born, you might want to order a couple of extra copies of the birth certificate for eventual use as identification. Make sure the official birth certificate is filled out accurately and check it over carefully before signing it.

CHAPTER FIVE

Who's Not Who

Tharmisdsbe Lurgy Prahustspondigfcem—what a name! A man named **Edward Hayes** decided to change his name to this colossal jawbreaker, thinking it would bring him luck.

Edward Hayes was granted permission to change his name because in America that is our privilege. In this country to be born with a name is not to be stuck with it.

Immigrants, of course, were the most zealous name-changers. They were not only permitted, but often encouraged to adopt a new name as soon as they arrived in this country. The majority did not make radical changes. Usually they simplified the spelling and anglicized difficult names to make them easier to pronounce.

It has also become customary for show business people to change their names. The following list of celebrities gives an idea of "who's not who."

Kareem Abdul-Jabbar (Ferdinand Lewis Alcindor, Jr.)

Woody Allen (Allen Stewart Konigsberg)

Julie Andrews (Julia Vernon)

Fred Astaire (Frederick Austerlitz)

Lauren Bacall (Betty Joan Perske)

Lucille Ball (Diane Belmont)

Orson Bean (Dallas Frederick Burrows)

Tony Bennett (Anthony Dominick Benedetto)

Jack Benny (Benjamin Kubelsky)

Irving Berlin (Israel Baline)

Yogi Berra (Lawrence Peter Berra)

Robert Blake (Michael James Vyencio Gubitosi)

David Bowie (David Jones)

Albert Brooks (Albert Einstein)

Mel Brooks (Melvin Kaminsky)

Yul Brynner (Taidge Kahn, Jr.)

Bugs Bunny (Happy Rabbit)

George Burns (Nathan Birnbaum)

Ellen Burstyn (Edna Roe Gillooly)

Michael Caine (Maurice Joseph Micklewhite)

Charo (Maria Rosaria Pilar Martinez Molina Baeza)

Chevy Chase (Cornelius Crane Chase)
Chubby Checker (Ernest Evans)
Cher (Cherilyn La Pierre)
Mike Connors (Krekor Ohanian)
Robert Conrad (Conrad Robert Falk)
Alice Cooper (Vincent Damon Furnier)
Elvis Costello (Declan Patrick McManus)
Joan Crawford (Lucille Le Seur)
Bing Crosby (Harry Lillis Crosby)
Tony Curtis (Bernard Schwartz)
Rodney Dangerfield (John Cohen)
John Denver (Henry John Deutschendorf, Jr.)
Bo Derek (Cathy Collins)
Dale Evans (Francis Octavia Smith)
Jamie Farr (Jaemeel Farah)
W.C. Fields (William Claude Dukenfield)
Gerald Rudolph Ford (Leslie Lynch King, Jr. — before adoption)
Redd Foxx (John Elroy Sanford)
Zsa Zsa Gabor (Sari Gabor)
Greta Garbo (Greta Luisa Gustafson)
Judy Garland (Frances Gumm)
James Garner (James Baumgarner)
Crystal Gayle (Brenda Gail Webb)
Halston (Roy Halston Frowick)
O. Henry (William Sidney Porter)
Englebert Humperdinck (Arnold Dorsey)
Elton John (Reginald Kenneth Dwight)

Tom Jones (Thomas Jones Woodward)
Boris Karloff (William Henry Pratt)
Danny Kaye (David Kaniel Kaminsky)
Diane Keaton (Diane Hall)
Ann Landers (Esther Pauline Friedman)
Michael Landon (Eugene Maurice Orowitz)
Jerry Lewis (Joseph Levitch)
Liberace (Wladziu Valentino Liberace)
Sophia Loren (Sophia Scicoloni)
Peter Lorre (Lazlo Lowenstein)
Karl Malden (Mladen Sekulovich)
Dean Martin (Dino Crocetti)
The Marx Brothers — Chico, Groucho, Gummo, Harpo and Zeppo (Leonard, Julius, Milton, Arthur and Herbert)
Meatloaf (Marvin Lee Aday)
Dina Merrill (Nedenia Hutton)
Rita Moreno (Rosita Dolores Alverio)
Pelé (Edson Arantes de Mascimento)
Harold Robbins (Francis Kane)
Roy Rogers (Leonard Sly)
Mickey Rooney (Joe Yule, Jr.)
Yves St. Laurent (Henri Donat Mathieu)
Soupy Sales (Milton Hines)
Sissy Spacek (Mary Elizabeth Spacek)
Sylvester Stallone (Michael Sylvester Stallone)
Barbara Stanwyck (Ruby Stevens)

Danny Thomas (Amos Jacobs)
Tiny Tim (Herbert Buckingham Khaury)
Rip Torn (Elmore Torn, Jr.)
Abigail Van Buren (Pauline Esther Friedman)
Nancy Walker (Ann Myrtle Swoyer)
John Wayne (Marion Michael Morrison)
Raquel Welch (Raquel Tejada)

Tuesday Weld (Susan Kerr Weld)
Gene Wilder (Jerome Silberman)
Flip Wilson (Clerow Wilson)
Shelley Winters (Shirley Schrift)
Stevie Wonder (Steveland Morris Hardaway)
Natalie Wood (Natasha Gurdin)
Jane Wyman (Sara Jane Fulks)
Anson Williams (Anson William Heimlick)

CHAPTER SIX

The Hall of Names

There are remarkable records, laws, coincidences and facts having to do with names. While the future is up to you, here is some intriguing information about the past.

• **Adolf...** in pre-war Germany, policemen, peddlers, and farmers were forbidden to call their horses by this name.

• **Barney...** is the name of an award given to cartoonists. It is taken from the comic strip, **Barney Google** and **Snuffy Smith.**

• **Borbon...** the great-great grandson of Carlos III of Spain, Don Alfonso de **Borbon y Borbon** (1866-1934), had 89 Christian names, of which several were lengthened by hyphenation.

• **Brown...** In 1974, Mr. Brian Brown of Wolverhampton, England, had his daughter christened **Maria Sullivan Corbett Fitzsimmons Jeffries Hart Burns Johnson Willard Dempsey Tunney Schmeling Sharkey Carnera Baer Braddock Louis Charles Walcott Marciano Patterson Johansson Liston Clay Frazier Foreman Brown.** He added, "I hope she will marry a boxer."

• **George D. Bryson...** stopped in Louisville, Kentucky on his way to New York. He registered at the Brown Hotel, and was assigned Room 307. Just as a lark, he stepped up to the desk and asked if there was any mail for him. Much to his amazement, he was handed a letter addressed to Mr. George D. Bryson, Room 307. It turned out that the preceding resident of the room was **another** George D. Bryson. The two Brysons eventually met so that they could revel over the incredible coincidence.

• **Chang...** is the most common family name in the world. A conservative estimate reports some 75,000,000 Chinese people named Chang.

- **Charlotte**...was the name of the German poet Schiller's three great loves— **Charlotte von Wolzogen, Charlotte von Kalb,** and **Charlotte von Lengefeld.**

- **Elizabeth, Mary** and **Ann**...accounted for about half of the girls' names for over three centuries.

- **En-lil-ti**...is believed to be the oldest surviving personal name in human history. It was discovered on a Sumerian tablet outside Baghdad.

- **Hannah**...is a "palindrome"—that is, a name spelled the same forward or backward.

- **Ike**...the nickname of **Dwight Eisenhower** was shortened from another nickname, **Ugly Ike.**

- **Kielbasa** (Sausage) and **Piwko** (Small Beer)...are just two of the names responsible for a law being passed in Poland, allowing people to drop their humiliating names.

- **Lana**...was the American name adopted by **Svetlana Alliluyeva,** the daughter of **Joseph Stalin,** when she became an American citizen in 1978.

- **M', Mc or Mac**...there are estimated to be 1,600,000 persons in Britain with M', Mc or Mac (Gaelic "son of") as part of their surnames. The commonest of these is Macdonald which accounts for about 55,000 of the Scottish population.

- **McAtee**...Mr. R. B. McAtee of Arlington, Virginia has collected 334 versions of the spelling of his family name since 1902. The Zulu ruler, Mzilikazi (born c.1795) had his name chronicled in 325 spellings.

- **O**...the single-letter surname O, of which 28 examples appear in Belgian telephone directories, is the commonest single-letter name.

- **Oliver**...was not used in England as a given name for a century after the death of the much-feared Lord Protector Oliver Cromwell.

- **Oscar**...is the gold plated statuette awarded annually to people in the film industry. Margaret Herrick, arriving for her first day of work as librarian of the Academy of Motion Picture Arts and Sciences, saw the nameless statuette and exclaimed, "He reminds me of my Uncle Oscar." The name stuck.

- **Sergius...** was a 9th Century Pope who initiated the practice of having each elected Pope adopt a new name. His original name was **Boca de Porco** (Pig's Mouth).

- **Smith...** The commonest surname in the English-speaking world is Smith. There are 659,050 nationally insured Smiths in Great Britain, of whom 10,102 are plain John Smith, and another 19,502 are John plus one or more given-name Smiths. Including uninsured persons, there are over 800,000 Smiths in England and Wales alone. There were an estimated 2,382,509 Smiths in the United States in 1973.

- **Touissant...** is a French name meaning *tous les saints* (all the saints). French parents give their children this name when they wish to honor all the saints.

- **Useless...** was the boyhood nickname of **Ulysses S. Grant.**

- **Adolph Blaine Charles David Earl Frederick Gerald Hubert Irvin John Kenneth Lloyd Martin Nero Oliver Paul Quincy Randolph Sherman Thomas Uncas Victor William Xerxes Yancy Zeus Wolfeschlegelsteinhausenbergdorf, Senior,** is the longest name on record.

- **Archimedes Zzzyandottie...** is the man listed last in the New York City telephone directory.

CHAPTER SEVEN

Going Through Customs

A World of Names

If you think there's no such name as **Yuk, Afi, Tal, Junko,** think again. For every **John** and **Mary** in the U.S.A., there's a **Chung** and **Ling** in China, and a **Claus** and **Elsa** in Germany.

For reasons of ancestral ties or the mere romance of a foreign-sounding name, you may wish to take a quick whirl around the world and look at some of the different names and naming customs.

AFRICANS

• A name that describes your husband's faults? This is the baby-naming practice among some mothers in Sudanese tribes.
• When a baby cries continually, some African tribes take it to mean the baby is wrongly named. Then they ask the doctor to select a name for the baby.
• Popular African names are: **Ashanti, Ayana, Camisha, Jomo, Kymer, Masika, Oto, Tanisha.**

AMERICAN INDIANS

• Being close to nature and unusually observant about natural phenomena, Indians imaginatively create names for their offspring. And, anything goes! **Tiponya** means, *"great horned owl sticking her head under her body and poking an egg that is hatching."* **Lokni** means *"rain coming through a small hole in the roof."*

• Some other popular American Indian names are: **Algoma, Chilali, Doba, Kulya, Malila, Onatah, Raini, Sipatu.**

ARABS AND MUSLIMS

• The *"99 Qualities of God,"* listed in the Koran, are used as standard, popular Arabic names, usually preceded by **Abdul, Abdel** or **Abd** which means *"servant of."*
• Muslim names generally come from the Prophet Muhammad *(the most popular name in the world)*, and from his descendants or immediate family. (Announce a telephone call for "Muhammad" at a Cousin's Club meeting in Saudi Arabia and most of the men will run to the phone.)
• Familiar Arabic names close to those in the Old Testament: **Dawud** *(David),* **Ibrahim** *(Abraham),* **Musa** *(Moses),* **Sara** *(Sarah),* **Sulaiman** *(Solomon)* and **Yusef** *(Joseph).*
• Popular Arabic girls' names include: **Aziza, Hatima, Indihar, Nabila, Nima** and **Rema.**

BRAZILIANS

• Given names are more important than family names. In fact, the surname can be legally changed, but **not** the given name. In Portuguese-speaking Brazil, typical girls' names are: **Ana, Emilia, Joano, Maria** and **Tereza.**
• For boys: **Antonio, Joao, Joaquim, Jorge, Jose** and **Manuel.**

CHINESE

• Parents will match first and middle names to form a beautiful image *(Heaven's Jewel).* Each child that follows will also be matched *(Heaven's Flower, Heaven's Gate* and so on).
• Some common boys' names are: **Chung, Fai, Hung, Kong** and **Tung.**
• For girls: **Lai, Lin, Ling, Mei** and **Ping.**

FRENCH

- The law used to demand that children be registered with historical French names spelled in the traditional way. All that changed in 1966 when the law was repealed.
- Popular boys' names: **Andre, Bernard, Bruno, Daniel, Eduard, Jacque, Jean, Paul** and **Rene.**
- For girls, **Brigitte, Danielle, Denise, Francoise, Michelle, Martine** and **Nicole.**

GERMANS

- Common boys' names: **Claus, Ernst, Friedrich, Heinz, Johann, Karl, Ludwig, Max, Peter, Werner** and **Wolfgang.**
- For girls: **Berta, Elsa, Frida, Gertrud, Gretchen, Heidi, Hildegard, Luise, Magda** and **Marta.**

GREEKS

- Male children are named after saints. Their middle name is their father's given name in a form meaning *"son of."*
- Popular boys' names are: **Christos, Constantine, Dimitri, Nicholas, Panayotis, Yannis** and **Yeorgi.**
- For girls: **Christina, Constance, Demetra, Helen, Nicholette** and **Sophia.**

IRISH

- The Irish favor the common Saints' names *(John, Michael, Patrick, Thomas)* as well as older Gaelic names *(Sean, Liam, Maire).*
- Popular boys' names are: **Brandon, Colin, Curran, Kevin** and **Seamus.**
- For girls: **Colleen, Fiona, Fianna, Kathleen, Maureen, Megan, Patricia** and **Tara.**

ISRAELIS

- Jewish children are traditionally named after some near relative who has passed away. Children are also named for famous Jews, showing the parents' pride in their ancestry.
- Popular Hebrew names for boys are: **Avrohom, Amon, Chaim, Gilad, Lael, Moshe, Nimrod, Shelomo, Yaakov, Zevie** and **Zvi.**
- For girls: **Atalia, Chava, Elana, Gilah, Haya, Michal, Nirah, Peninah, Tikvah** and **Ziona.**

ITALIANS

- Italians like the names of historical rulers and heroes.
- For boys: **Amadeo, Carlo, Enrico, Francesco, Giuseppi, Lorenzo, Luigi, Mario, Pietro, Umberto, Vincenzo** and **Vittorio.**
- For girls: **Amelia, Angela, Bianca, Francesca, Lucia, Maria, Rosa** and **Teresa.**

JAPANESE

- Names of *"virtue"* are given to girls (**Yoshi**—*good;* **Michi**—*righteous).* Boys are often named for numbers—usually denoting the order of birth (**Taro**—*first;* **Jiro**—*second).*
- Popular boys' names are: **Akira, Hiroshi, Kenji, Tadashi, Takeo** and **Yoshio.**
- For girls: **Hiroko, Junko, Masako, Michiko, Reiko, Sachiko, Toshiko** and **Yoahiko.**

SCANDINAVIANS

- In Denmark, Norway and Sweden, traditional names for boys are: **Anders, Anton, Arne, Bjorn, Eric, Gustaf, Harald, Henrik, Jens, Jorgen, Knut, Lars, Leif, Olaf, Soren** and **Ulric.**
- For girls: **Agna, Asta, Astrid, Dorothea, Elisa, Else, Eva, Frederika, Gunda, Hedvig, Ingrid, Karin, Kirsten, Kristina, Signe, Sigrid** and **Thea.**

SPANISH

- The common names in Spanish-speaking countries including Mexico, Spain, Central and South America are those of Catholic saints.
- Common names for boys are: **Alfonso, Enrique, Jesus, Juan, Julio, Luis** and **Pedro.**
- For girls: **Alicia, Carmen, Cecilia, Juana** and **Rosa.**

AROUND THE WORLD WITH JOHN!

John is the most common name in the western world. Here's the way John looks in 24 languages:

Arabic	Hanna	**Irish**	Sean, Shane
Belgian	Jan, Jehan	**Italian**	Giovanni
Bulgarian	Ivan	**Norwegian**	Hohan, Jens
Czech	Jan	**Polish**	Jan, Iwan
Danish	Hans, Jan	**Portuguese**	Joao
Finnish	Hannes	**Rumanian**	Ioan
French	Jean	**Russian**	Ivan
Gaelic	Jan	**Scotch**	Ian
German	Johannes, Hans	**Spanish**	Juan, Joao
Greek	Ioannes	**Swedish**	Jonam, Jens
Hebrew	Yohanan	**Turkish**	Ohannes
Hungarian	Janos	**Yiddish**	Yochanan

CHAPTER EIGHT

They're Playing Our Song

Wouldn't it be loverly for your child to have a song associated with his or her name?

Thousands of songs are written about someone. Here's a list of songs containing names. Perhaps it will help you make your selection.

Sweet Adeline
Alexander's Ragtime Band
Alfie
Alice Blue Gown
Once In Love With Amy
Anastasia
Annie's Song
Barney Google
Bess You Is My Woman
Betty Co-Ed
My Girl Bill
(He's Just My) Bill
Candida
Candy
Sweet Caroline
Cecilia
Sweet Charity
Chloe
Clair
Oh My Darling Clementine
Corina, Corina

Daisey, Daisey
Daniel
Delta Dawn
Delilah
Diane
Dominique
Dinah
Hello Dolly
Elvira
Emilia Polka
Emily
Fanny
Fernando
Blow, Gabriel, Blow
Sweet Genevieve
Georgy Girl
Gigi
Gloria
Hard Hearted Hannah
I'm Just Wild About Harry
Dance With Me, Henry

Hernando's Hideaway
Honey
Ida, Sweet As Apple Cider
Goodnight Irene
Lady Jane
Jean
Jeanie With The Light Brown Hair
Jennifer Juniper
Jesse
Jezebel
Jim (Never Sends Me Pretty Flowers)
Joanne
Joey
Johnny B. Goode
Josephine
Hey, Jude
Julia
I Wish I Could Shimmy Like
   My Sister Kate
O Katharina
K-K-K-Katy
Lara's Theme
Sweet Leilani
Lily Of The Valley
Linda
Lola
Sweet Lorraine
Lucille
Lucy In the Sky With Diamonds
Lulu's Back In Town
Lydia, The Tattooed Lady
Mack The Knife
When You And I Were Young, Maggie
Mame
Mandy
Maria

Marian the Librarian
Marie
Mary Is A Grand Old Name
Melinda
Michael, Row The Boat Ashore
Michelle
Thoroughly Modern Millie
Minnie The Moocher
Nadia's Theme
Nancy With The Laughing Face
No, No Nanette
Wait Till The Sun Shines, Nellie
Oliver
Hey Paula
Rikki Don't Lose That Number
Rosalie
Gypsy Rose
My Wild Irish Rose
Rambling Rose
Lovely Rita
Rosie, You Are My Posie
Ruby
Rudolph The Red Nosed Reindeer
Sadie, Sadie, Married Lady
My Gal Sal
Lovin' Sam (The Shiek of Alabam)
Stella By Starlight
Sweet Sue
Sunny
Oh Susanna
If You Knew Susie
Tammy
Tara's Theme
My Funny Valentine
Zorba's Theme

CHAPTER NINE

Your Little Star and the Stars

Astro-Logical Signs

We aren't going to chart your baby's birthdate. We are going to give you an idea of the general character traits for children born under each of the twelve Zodiac signs. In addition to each astrological sign, every month has its own birthstone and flower. Look at the lists. It's fun to see what applies to your baby. The astrological new year begins with—

Your ARIES Baby
March 21 to April 20
The Ram

The Aries baby will let you know he's around. He'll raise his hand before the teacher asks the question. He's a hardy little guy and will probably be a captain of a team.

Your TAURUS Baby
April 21 to May 21
The Bull

The Taurus baby is a cuddler. She'll fuss and fret but is sure to be soothed by the warmth and security of your touch. She adores being held, hugged and swaddled in soft blankets.

Your GEMINI Baby
May 22 to June 21
The Twins

The Gemini baby starts babbling at a very early age. Her curiosity is endless and, to keep her happy, you'll want to adorn her crib with lots of colorful objects for her little eyes to track.

Your CANCER Baby
June 22 to July 23
The Crab

The Cancer baby often changes his mood in a flash. He is a born collector of everything and anything. When he's old enough, give him a brightly colored box for him to store his many treasures.

Your LEO Baby
July 24 to August 23
The Lion

The Leo baby will dazzle and charm visitors. He's a born actor and loves being the center of attention—and usually is. Later he'll surprise you with his creativity. It's the Leo child who will be the life of the party.

Your VIRGO Baby
August 24 to September 23
The Virgin

The Virgo baby likes to be neat and clean. Change her often and you'll keep her gurgling and cooing. It's the Virgo child who cleans her room without being asked and does her homework without being reminded.

Your LIBRA Baby
September 24 to October 23
Balance

The Libra baby loves people. She's usually surrounded by doting members of the family who are drawn by her magnetic personality. She'll gladly climb into the lap of Aunt Tessie and give her her most winning smile.

Your SCORPIO Baby
October 24 to November 22
The Scorpion

The Scorpio baby has charisma. He'll win your heart from the moment his eyes gaze at you and appear to look deep into your soul. It's the Scorpio child who collects lizards and snakes and all the family secrets.

Your SAGITTARIUS Baby
November 23 to December 21
The Archer

The Sagittarius baby is a spunky, good natured little gal. She's a born comedian and her infectious laughter will start early and stay forever. She loves to travel. Just strap her in the car seat and go.

Your CAPRICORN Baby
December 22 to January 20
The Goat

The Capricorn baby is a born diplomat. He loves to be around grown-ups, especially Grandma. He's most likely to go through Mommy's dresser drawer or poke around in Daddy's desk.

Your AQUARIUS Baby

January 21 to February 19
The Water Bearer

Don't be surprised if your Aquarius baby constantly surprises you. This little one changes daily and just when you think you've got her figured out—bingo! She's changed.

Your PISCES Baby

February 20 to March 20
The Fish

The Pisces baby is sweet and sensitive. Place him in a canopy crib, surround him with plush toys and gently rock him to sleep. He is super-sensitive and may know your thoughts even before you are aware of them.

Birthstones and Flowers

MONTH	BIRTHSTONE	FLOWER
January	Garnet	Carnation
February	Amethyst	Violet
March	Bloodstone	Jonquil
April	Diamond	Sweet Pea
May	Emerald	Lily of the Valley
June	Pearl	Rose
July	Ruby	Larkspur
August	Sardonyx	Gladiolus
September	Sapphire	Aster
October	Opal	Calendula
November	Topaz	Chrysanthemum
December	Turquoise	Poinsettia

CHAPTER TEN

Numerology and Names

Playing the Numbers

The Greek philosopher, Pythagoras, worked out a theory of numbers. He believed all human history could be divided into cycles. He measured those cycles with the numbers from one to nine. Modern numerology says that these numbers reflect the cycles of history and of individual lives. So, numerology uses a formula to reduce important data – names, dates, etc. – to these numbers.

Numerology is fun and a fascinating subject. For those of you who share a passing interest, here's a simplified explanation of how to test the names you're considering for your baby.

Every letter has its own value.

A	B	C	D	E	F	G	H	I	J	K	L	M	N	O	P	Q	R	S	T	U	V	W	X	Y	Z
1	2	3	4	5	6	7	8	9	1	2	3	4	5	6	7	8	9	1	2	3	4	5	6	7	8

Write down the names you've been considering for your baby; first, middle, and your last name. Then write the corresponding number under each letter of the complete name. Add it up and get the total. You'll get a two-digit number. Add those two numbers together to get a number from one to nine.

```
A N D R E W     S H E R M A N     P I N K H A M
1 5 4 9 5 5     1 8 5 9 4 1 5     7 9 5 2 8 1 4

    29       +        33       +         36

          98  =  17  =  8

      9 + 8 = 17    1 + 7 = 8
```

Andrew Sherman Pinkham is an "8".

Once you've figured out the name's numbers, refer to the following inter-
pretations:

"1"... **Numero Uno**—Powerful One. Creative leaders.

"2"... **Two-getherness.** Friendly, sociable. Great mixers and followers.

"3"... **Good things come in threes**... the artistic and inspired ones.

"4"... **Four he's a jolly good fellow.** Boy Scouts, Girl Scouts—dependable,
honest, trustworthy.

"5"... **Five and alive.** The most fascinating ones. Fun to have around, if they'll
stay around long enough.

"6"... **Six of one, half dozen of the other.** Spiritual leaders, intellectual leaders. Deep, sincere, scholarly, with strong social consciences.

"7"... **Lucky sevens have the smarts.** Their intellect pays off for them.

"8"... **Eight is Enough**... to organize and plan and drive themselves as well
as others. They get the job done.

"9"... **Nine is fine!** The vibration of "Nine" is from the heart. They believe in
and fight for justice and righteousness.

CHAPTER ELEVEN

Ta-Dummmmmmmm!

Birth Announcements

You've selected a name for your new baby. Now it's time to introduce him or her. We hope the following suggestions will spark your imagination and help you with an original birth announcement.

Announcements Based On Last Names

Use your last name to come up with a clever and unique announcement. The **Warners** announce a double feature (the birth of twins); the **Ushers** give their newborn babe a front row seat; the **Freys** have a small fry; the **Watts** announce "some very illuminating news about the light of their lives."

Announcements Based On Occupations

What's your line? Could it be the basis for your birth announcement? Jewelers produce a little gem; grocers advertise a mid-week special; the owners of a mail order business send out a little first class male; the mailman announces his special delivery.

Announcements Based On Interests

How about some hobby or pastime you can build on? Scrabble enthusiasts spell out the baby's vital statistics on a game board; crossword puzzle lovers solve a new puzzle; sailing enthusiasts announce a new arrival into port; avid theatre-goers use a program announcing the new production, starring their newborn.

Announcements Based On Locale

What about your city or state, or even the street where you live? Do they spark some ideas?

An Australian couple announce the joy that has just "hopped into their lives." (The card they send out is in the shape of a kangaroo with all the details imprinted on the baby kangaroo in the mother's pouch.) A Texas couple announce a cowpuncher who has lassoed their hearts. Georgians send out their news in a nutshell. Philadelphians announce the arrival of a little Brotherly Love.

Designing The Announcements

Once you have an idea in mind for your baby's birth announcement, you're ready for the second part of the creative process: designing the announcement. That decision should be based on your artistic talent and the time and the money you want to spend.

There are lots of options open to you. The simplest is line art or photographs used with a typewritten or handwritten message. These can be done individually or, your prototype can be taken to a local printer for reproduction in quantity.

If you are on a tight budget, here are some "crafty" ideas: block printing; thumb print art; potato prints; silhouettes; paper cutouts; miniature collages using fabrics and buttons and bows.

There are wonderful arts and crafts books at most local libraries as well as your local book stores and art supply stores. Or, consult *We Are Proud To Announce*, a fine book on birth announcements, published by Redbook Publishing Co., 230 Park Avenue, New York, N.Y. 10017.

Now you're ready to design your very own masterpiece.

CHAPTER TWELVE

Naming Names

An Introduction to More Than 10,000 Names

Our goal is to give you the widest possible choice of names for your baby.

Up to now, other baby name books have simply listed thousands upon thousands of names without giving any guidance on how to select your favorites. And, when you've finished looking through them, you're back to where you started ... **NAMELESS!**

The name listings consist of the following elements:

Main Entry. This is the most common American usage and spelling.

Origins and Meanings. Care has been taken to find the correct origins and meanings. In some cases we've added a little history of the name. Although we feel these should have little influence on your choice, it's fun information to know.

Variations. These are names derived from the main entry, nicknames and alternate spellings. We also show you variations of the main entry from different countries around the world.

We've provided a format that's easy to use and is a real tool in helping you select the best name.

As you go through the list, you will find a box beside each entry. When you find a name that you like, put a check mark in the box. If you happen to like a variation of that name, circle it.

When you've finished, you'll have lots of names you **REALLY LIKE!**
Now get to it ... have some fun ... and GOOD LUCK!!!

Name Me, I'm Your Son!

Most Popular "A" Name.... **ANDREW**

☐ **AARON** *(Hebrew, "Exalted")*. The brother of Moses and the first high priest of the Jews who led the Israelites out of Egypt/ The Arab Caliph Haroun-al-Raschid was immortalized in the Arabian Nights.
ARI, ARON Arabic: HAROUN; Hebrew: AHARON.

☐ **ABBIE/ABBEY** See ABNER, ABBOTT.

☐ **ABBOTT** *(Arabic, "Father")*. From the Aramaic Abba meaning a father/ The modern usage comes from the heads of religious orders called abbotts.
ABBA, ABBIE, ABBEY, ABBY Spanish: ABAD.

☐ **ABDUL** *(Arabic, "Son of")*.

☐ **ABNER** *(Hebrew, "Father of light")*.
ABBEY, ABBIE, AVNER.

☐ **ABRAHAM** *(Hebrew, "Father of a multitude")*. With his wife Sarah, the founder of the Hebrew race in 2,000 B.C.
ABE, ABEY, ABIE, ABRAM Italian: ABRAMO; Spanish: ABRAHAN; Dutch: BRAM; Russian: AVRAAM; Arabic: IBRAHIM; Greek: ARAM.

☐ **ABRAM** *(Hebrew, "Exalted father")*.
ABE, ABIE, ABRAHAM (See ABRAHAM).

☐ **ACE** *(Latin, "Unity")*.

☐ **ACKLEY** *(Old English, "From the oak-meadow")*.
ACKERLEY.

☐ **ADAIR** *(Scotch, "From the oak-tree ford")*.

☑ **ADAM** *(Hebrew, "Man of the red*

earth"). The biblical Adam was created by God from the red earth/ This name was not used until it was adopted by the Celts.
ADAMS, ADAN, ADDISON, ADDY, ADE, EDAM Italian: ADAMO.

☐ **ADDISON** (Old English, "Son of Adam"). See ADAM.

☐ **ADLAI** (Hebrew, "Witness of Jehovah").

☐ **ADOLPH** (Old German, "Noble wolf"). A name once popular with German nobility and royalty/ Several saints bear this name.
DOLPH, DOLPHUS French: ADOLPHE; Italian/Spanish: ADOLFO; Swedish: ADOLPHUS.

☐ **ADON** (Phoenician, "Lord"). A Hebrew name for Jehovah/ In Greek mythology Adonis was a young god loved by Aphrodite.
Greek: ADONIS.

☐ **ADRIAN** (Latin, "The black one"). Six Popes were named Adrian including the only Englishman.
HADRIAN French: ADRIEN; Italian: ADRIANO.

☐ **ADRIEL** (Hebrew, "Of God's flock").

☐ **AHMAD/AHMED** (Arabic, "Most high"). One of the many names for Mohammad.

☐ **AIKEN** (Anglo-Saxon, "The oaken").

☐ **AINSLEY** (Old English, "From the oak meadow").

☐ **AJAX** (Greek, "Eagle").

☐ **ALADDIN** (Arabic, "The height of religion"). The hero of the Arabian Nights.

☐ **ALAN** (Irish, "Handsome," "Harmony").
AL, ALLEN French: ALAIN; Italian/Spanish: ALANO.

☐ **ALASTAIR** See ALEXANDER.

☐ **ALBAN** (Latin, "White"). Saint Alban was the first British martyr.
ALBION, ALBIN, AUBIN Spanish: ALBA, ALVA.

☐ **ALBERN** (Old German, "Noble bear").

☐ **ALBERT** (Old German, "Noble bright"). The name of saints, emperors and the husband of Queen Victoria.
ADALBERT, ADELBERT, AL, BERT, BERTY, DELBERT, ELBERT, ETHELBERT Latin: ALBERTUS: French: AUBERT; Italian/Spanish: ALBERTO, ALBERTINO; German: ALBRECHT, ULBRECHT.

☐ **ALDEN** (Old English, "Old friend").
AL, ALDIN, ALDWIN, ALWIN, ELDEN.

□ **ALDER** *(Old English, "The alder tree")*. From the same name group as Elder and Older/ The Alder tree was a symbol of authority.
ELDER.

□ **ALDIS** *(Old English, "From the old house")*. Aldous Huxley, writer.
ALDOUS, ALDUS.

□ **ALDOUS** See ALDIS.

□ **ALDRED** *(Old English, "Old counsel")*.
ELDRED, ELDREDGE Norwegian: ELDRID.

□ **ALDRICH** *(Old English, "Old king")*.
AL, ALDRIC, ALDRIDGE, ELDRIC French: AUDRIC (See ELDRIDGE).

□ **ALDWIN** See ALDEN.

□ **ALEC** See ALEXANDER.

□ **ALERON** *(Latin, "The winged")*.

□ **ALEXANDER** *(Greek, "Defender of man")*. In addition to Alexander the Great, eight popes and many kings, emperors and czars bore this name.
ALEC, ALEX, ALEXIS, ALICK, SANDOR, SANDY French: ALEXANDRE, ALEXIS; Italian: ALLESANDRO, SANDRO, ALLESIO; Spanish: ALEJANDRO, ALEJO; Russian: ALESCHA, ALEXEI, SASCHA; Scotch: ALAISTAIR, ALISTAIR, ALISTER, ALLISTER, SANDERS, SAUNDERS; Greek: ALEXANDROS, ALEXIOS.

□ **ALFONSO** See ALPHONSO.

□ **ALFORD** *(Old English, "From the old ford")*.

□ **ALFRED** *(Old English, "Wise counsel")*. King Alfred the Great, reputedly England's wisest and most compassionate ruler, freed his country from the Danes in the 9th Century.
AL, ALF, ALFIE, ELFRED, FRED, FREDDIE Italian/Spanish: **ALFREDO**.

□ **ALGER** *(Old German, "Noble spearman")*.
AL, ELGAR.

□ **ALGERNON** *(Old French, "With whiskers")*.
AL

□ **ALI** *(Arabic, "Most exalted")*.

□ **ALISTAIR** See ALASTAIR.

☒ **ALLAN/ALLEN** See ALAN.

□ **ALLARD** *(Old English, "Sacred and brave")*.
AL French: ALARD.

□ **ALLISTER** See ALASTAIR.

□ **ALONSO** See ALPHONZO.

□ **ALPHEUS** *(Hebrew, "Substitute")*.

□ **ALPHONSO** *(Old German, "Of a noble family")*. Five Spanish kings bore this name at the height of Spain's greatness.
ALF, ALFIE, LON, LONNY, FONS, FONZ, FONZIE French: **ALPHONSE;** Italian: **ALFONSO;** Spanish: **ALONSO, ALONZO;** German: **ALFONS.**

□ **ALSTON** *(Old English, "Noble estate")*.

□ **ALTON** *(Old English, "From the old town")*.

□ **ALVA** See ALBAN.

□ **ALVAH** *(Hebrew, "Exalted")*.

□ **ALVIN** *(Old German, "Nobel friend")*. Sergeant Alvin York, WWI hero.
ALFAN, ALVY Italian/Spanish: **ALUINO;** German: **ALWIN.**

□ **ALVIS** *(Old Norse, "All wise")*. In Norse mythology the dwarf Alviss desired to marry the daughter of Thor.
ELVIS.

□ **AMADORE** *(Italian, "Lover")*.
French: **AMAND;** Italian: **AMANDO.**

□ **AMBROSE** *(Greek, "The divine, immortal one")*. Ambrosia, the food of the Greek gods, brought them immortality/ The 4th century Saint Ambrose of Milan/ In 1961 Saint Ambrose was designated the patron saint of educational television.
French: **ABROISE;** Italian: **AMBROGIO;** Spanish: **AMBROSIO;** German: **AMBROSIUS.**

□ **AMIAS** See AMADEUS.

□ **AMEL** *(Hebrew, "He who is god")*.

□ **AMORY** *(Old German, "Divine rule")*.
AMERY.

□ **AMOS** *(Hebrew, "Bearer of the burden")*. A biblical prophet.

□ **AMUND** *(Teutonic, "Great protector")*.

□ **ANDREW** *(Greek, "Strong," "Manly")*. One of the Apostles/ Patron saint of Scotland and Russia/ Andrew Jackson, 7th president of the U.S./ Andrew Carnegie, Industrialist/ Andres Segovia, guitar virtuoso/ Andre Gide, winner of Nobel Prize in literature.
ANDY French: **ANDRE, ANDRIEN;** Italian: **ANDREA;** Spanish: **ANDRES;** Danish: **ANDERS;** German: **ANDREAS;** Russian: **ANDREIAN;** Greek: **ANDREAS.**

□ **ANGELO** *(Italian, "Angel")*.
ANGEL French: **ANGE;** Italian: **ANGIOLO;** German: **ENGEL;** Greek: **ANGELOS.**

□ **ANGUS** *(Scotch, "The choice")*.

The Irish god of love, youth, and beauty.
GUS.

☐ **ANNAS** *(Hebrew, Masc. of Anna, "The Lord's grace")*.

☐ **ANSEL** See ANSELM.

☐ **ANSELM** *(Old German, "Divine helmet")*. St. Anselm founded the philosophical school of scholasticism.
ANSEL French: ANSELME; Italian: ANSELMO; Greek: ANSO.

☐ **ANSLEY** *(Old English, "From the meadow")*.

☐ **ANSON** *(Old English, "Nobleman's son")*.
HANSON.

☐ **ANTHONY** *(Latin, "Of inestimable value")*. St. Anthony is the patron saint of Italy and of young children/ The great Roman Emperor Marc Antony was the lover of Cleopatra.
ANTONY, ANTONE, TONY French: ANTOINE; Italian: TONIO; German: ANTON; Swiss: TONI; Slovak: ANTONIN.

☐ **ARCHER** *(Old English, "Bowman, archer")*.

☐ **ARCHIBALD** *(German, "Noble and bold")*.
ARCH, ARCHER, ARCHIE, ARCHY

French: **ARCHAMBAULT**; Italian: **ARCIBALDO**; German: **ARCHIMBALD**.

☐ **ARCHIE** See ARCHIBALD.

☐ **ARDEL** *(Old English, "From the valley")*.

☐ **ARDEN** *(Latin, "Ardent")*.
ARDIN.

☐ **ARGUS** *(Greek, "Vigilant")*. In Greek mythology Argus was the son of Zeus/ Also a giant with a hundred eyes.

☐ **ARIEL** *(Hebrew, "Lion of God")*.

☐ **ARIES** *(Latin, "A ram")*.

☐ **ARISTOTLE** *(Greek, "Best of the thinkers")*. Ancient Greek philosopher/Aristotle Onassis, Greek shipping magnate.

☐ **ARLEN** *(Irish, "A pledge")*.

☐ **ARLEY** See HARLEY.

☐ **ARLO** See HARLOW.

☐ **ARMAND** *(Old German, "Soldier")*. The patron saint of the Netherlands.
ARMAN, ARMANDO (See HERMAN).

☐ **ARMSTRONG** *(Old English, "Strong arm")*.

☐ **ARNALL** *(Old German, "Gracious eagle")*.

43

☐ **ARNEY** (Old German, "Eagle").

☐ **ARNOLD** (Old German, "Strong as an eagle").
ARNIE, ARNY French: **ARNAUD, ARNAULT**; Italian: **ARNOLDO**; Spanish: **ARNALDO**; German: **AHRENT**.

☐ **ARTEMAS** (Greek, "Gift of Artemis"). The masculine form of Artemis, the Greek goddess of the hunt/ St. Artemas was one of St. Paul's disciples.
ARTEMUS, ARTIE, ARTY.

☐ **ARTHUR** (Welsh, "Noble"). King Arthur was the semi-legendary hero of the Knights of the Round Table.
ART, ARTIE, ARTUR French: **ARTUS**; Italian/Spanish: **ARTURO**.

☐ **ASHBY** (Old English, "Ash-tree farm").

☐ **ASHER** (Hebrew, "Happy"). Biblical, a son of Jacob.

☐ **ASHLEY** (Old English, "From the ash-tree meadow").

☐ **AUBREY** (Old French, "Elf ruler"). Aubrey Beardsley, English painter.
AVERY French: **AUBRI**; German: **ALBERICH**; Swedish: **ALBERIK**.

☐ **AUGUST** (Latin, "Majestic exalted). First bestowed as a title on Augustus Caesar by the Roman Senate, Augustus was later used by other Roman Emperors/ Auguste Renoir, French painter.
AUGIE, AUGUSTINE, AUGUSTUS, AUSTEN, AUSTIN, GUS, GUSTIN French: **AUGUSTIN, AUGUSTE**; Italian: **AGOSTINO**; Spanish: **AUGUSTIN**.

☐ **AUGUSTINE** See AUGUST.

☐ **AUSTIN** See AUGUST.

☐ **AVERELL** (Old English, "Boar-warrior"). Averell Harriman, American statesman.
AVERIL.

☐ **AVERY** See AUBREY.

☐ **AVRAM** See ABRAHAM.

☐ **AXEL** (Old German, "Father of peace").

☐ **AZIEL** (Hebrew, "God makes strong").

B Most Popular "B" Name....
BRIAN

☐ **BAILEY** (Latin, "Bailiff").
BAYLEY.

☐ **BALDWIN** (Old German, "Cou-

rageous friend"). French: **BAUDOIN;** Italian: **BALDOVINO, BALDUINO;** German: **BALDUIN.**

☐ **BALLARD** *(Old German, "Bold, strong").*

☐ **BALTHASAR** *(Greek, "May God protect the king").* One of the three Wise Men.
BALTHAZAR French: **BALTASARD;** Italian: **BALTASSARE;** Spanish: **BALTASAR;** Greek: **BALTASAROS;** Hebrew: **BELSHAZZAR.**

☐ **BANNING** *(Irish, "Little blond one").*

☐ **BARCLAY** *(Old English, "Birch meadow").*
BERKELEY.

☐ **BARD** *(Irish, "Poet and singer").* Bards also brought the news.
BART Scottish: **BAIRD.**

☐ **BARKER** *(Old English, "A tanner").*

☐ **BARLOW** *(Old English, "From the boar's hill").*

☐ **BARNABAS** *(Greek, "Son of exhortation").* St. Barnabas travelled with the apostle Paul/ In England he is known as St. Barnaby.
BARNABY, BARNEBAS Irish: **BARNEY.**

☐ **BARNARD** See **BERNARD.**

☐ **BARNETT** *(Old English, "Commander").*
BARNEY, BARRY.

☐ **BARNEY** See **BARNABAS, BARNETT, BERNARD.**

☐ **BARRET** *(Old German, "Bear-might").*

☐ **BARRY** *(Irish, "Spear," or "Pointed").*
BARRIE See **BARNETT, BARUCH, BERNARD.**

☐ **BART/BARTH** See **BARTHOLOMEW.**

☐ **BARTHOLOMEW** *(Hebrew, "Farmer's son").* St. Bartholomew was one of the twelve Apostles.
BART, BARTEL, BARTH, BARTHOL, BARTLET, BAT French: **BARTHOLOME;** Italian: **BORTOLO, BARTOLOMEO;** Spanish: **BARTOLOME;** Danish: **BARDO;** German: **BARTHEL, BARTHOLOMAUS, BARTOL, BERTEL;** Irish: **BARTLEY.**

☐ **BARTLEY** *(Old English, "Bart's meadow").*

☐ **BARTON** *(Old English, "From the barley farm").*
BART.

☐ **BAXTER** *(Old English, "A baker").*
BAX.

☐ **BAYARD** *(French, "A gentleman of honor and courage")*.
BAY Italian: BAIRADO.

☐ **BEAUREGARD** *(Old French, "Of a beautiful nature")*.
BEAU, BO.

☐ **BELA** *(Hebrew, "Destruction")*.

☐ **BELDON** *(Old English, "From the Beautiful valley")*.
BELDON.

☐ **BELLAMY** *(Latin, "Fine friend")*.

☐ **BEN** *(Hebrew, "Son")*. Also a short form of names beginning with "Ben".
BENNIE, BENNY. (See BENEDICT, BENJAMIN, BENTLEY, BENTON).

☐ **BENEDICT** *(Latin, "Blessed")*. St. Benedict founded the Benedictine order/ Fifteen popes were named Benedict/ Benito Juarez, 19th century president of Mexico.
BEN, BENDIX, BENNET, BENNETT, BENNY French: BENOIT; Italian: BENEDETTO; Spanish: BENEDICTO, BENITO; German: BENEDIKE, BENEDIKT, DIX; Swedish: BENGT; Swiss: BENZEL; Norwegian: BENEDIK, BENIKE; Slavic: BENKO.

☐ **BENJAMIN** *(Hebrew, "The son of the right hand")*. Jacob's youngest and favorite son who obeyed his father.
BEN, BENJI, BENNY Hebrew: BINYAMIN.

☐ **BENNET** See BENEDICT.

☐ **BENSON** *(English, "Son of Benjamin")*.
BEN, BENNY.

☐ **BENTLEY** *(Old English, "From the winding meadow")*.
BEN, BENNY.

☐ **BENTON** *(Old English, "From the winding town")*.
BEN, BENNY.

☐ **BEORN** *(Old German, "Bear")*.
Norwegian: BJORN.

☐ **BERKELEY** See BARCLAY.

☐ **BERN** *(Old German, "Bear")*.

☐ **BERNARD** *(German, "Bold as a bear")*. St. Bernard is the patron saint of mountain climbers/ Bernard Shaw, writer/ Bernard Baruch, advisor to presidents.
BARNARD, BARNEY, BARNIE, BERNIE, BERNY, BURNARD Italian/Spanish: BERNAL, BERNARDO; Dutch: BARENDT; German: BAREND, BENNO, BEREND, BERNHARD.

☐ **BERT** *(Old English, "Bright")*.
See ALBERT, BERTHOLD, BERTRAM, HERBERT and BURTON.

☐ **BERTHOLD** *(Old German, "Brilliant ruler")*. St. Berthold founded the Carmelite order.
BERT, BERTOLD.

□ **BERTON** See BURTON.

□ **BERTRAM** *(Old German, "Bright raven")*. Bertrand Russell, English philosopher and Nobel Prize winner for literature.
BERT, BERTY, BURT French: BERTRAND; Italian: BERTRANDO; Spanish: BELTRAN; Scotch: BARTHRAM.

□ **BEVAN** *(Irish, "Young archer")*. BEVIN.

□ **BILL** See WILLIAM.

□ **BING** *(Old German, "The kettle-shaped hollow")*.

□ **BINGHAM** *(Old Norse, "From the town where grain is stored")*.

□ **BIRCH** *(Old English, "The birch tree")*.
BIRK, BURCH.

□ **BISHOP** *(Old English, "The bishop")*.

□ **BJORN** See BEORN.

□ **BLAINE** *(Irish, "Thin")*.
BLANE, BLAYNE.

□ **BLAIR** *(Irish, "Marshy plain," Battlefield")*.

□ **BLAKE** *(Old English, "Light complected and fair-haired")*.
BLAKEY.

□ **BLANE** See BLAINE.

□ **BLAYNE** See BLAINE.

□ **BLAZE** *(Old German, "A brand")*. St. Blaze is the patron saint of wool manufacturers.
BLASE French: BLAISE; Italian: BACCIO; Spanish: BLAS; German: BLASI; Hungarian: BALAS.

□ **BO** See BEAUREGARD.

□ **BOB** See ROBERT.

□ **BODEN** *(Old Norse, "The ready one")*.

□ **BOGART** *(Danish, "Archer")*.
BO, BOGEY.

□ **BOND** *(Old English, "Tiller")*.
BONDY.

□ **BORIS** *(Slavic, "Warrior")*. Boris Godunov was a 17th century Russian czar/ Boris Pasternak, winner of Nobel Prize in literature.

□ **BOWEN** *(Welsh, "A youth")*.

□ **BOWIE** *(Irish, "Yellow-haired")*.

□ **BOYCE** *(Old French, "Living in the woods")*.

□ **BOYD** *(Irish, "Blond")*.
BOYDEN.

□ **BOZO** *(Old German, "Commander")*.

□ **BRAD** See BRADEN, BRADLEY, BRADFORD, BRADY.

☐ **BRADEN** *(Old English, "From the broad valley")*.
BRAD.

☐ **BRADFORD.** *(Old English, "From the broad river crossing")*.
BRAD.

☑ **BRADLEY** *(Old English, "From the broad meadow")*.
BRAD, LEE.

☐ **BRADY** *(Old English, "From the broad isle")*.
BRAD.

☐ **BRANDON** *(Old English, "From the flaming hill")*.
BRAN, BRAND, BRENDON.

☐ **BRANT** *(Old English, "Proud")*.
See BRAND, BRANDON.

☐ **BRENDAN** *(Irish Gaelic, "Sword")*. Brendan Behan, Irish playwright/ St. Brendan is the patron saint of sailors.
BREN, BRENDON.

☐ **BRENT** *(Old English, "The tall and erect")*.

☐ **BRENTON** *(Old English, "Steep hill")*.
BRENT.

☐ **BRETT** *(Celtic, "Native of Brittany")* Bret Harte, American writer.
BRET.

☐ **BREWSTER** *(Old English, "A brewer")*.
BREW.

☒ **BRIAN** *(Irish, "Strong")*. Brian Boru, 10th century A.D., the most famous of all Irish kings, was the subject of many ballads due to his heroism.
BRIANT, BRIEN, BRYAN, BRYANT Italian: BRIANO.

☐ **BRICE** *(Welsh, "The swift")*.
BRYCE.

☐ **BRIGHAM** *(Old English, "The home at the enclosed bridge")*. Brigham Young, Mormon leader.

☐ **BROCK** *(Old English, "A badger")*.

☐ **BRODERICK** *(Welsh, "Son of Roderick")*.
BROD, RICK (See RODERICK).

☐ **BRODIE** *(Irish, "Ditch")*. A noted Scottish clan name.

☐ **BRONSON** *(Old English, "Son of the brown one")*.
BRON.

☐ **BROOK** *(Old English, "From the brook")*.
BROOKS.

☐ **BRUCE** *(Old French, "From the brush")*. Robert Bruce was a 14th century king of Scotland and a national hero.

☐ **BRUNO** *(Italian, "Brown haired one")*.

☐ **BUCK** *(Old English, "Male deer")*.

☐ **BUDD** *(Old English, "Messenger")*.
BUD, BUDDY.

☐ **BURDON** *(Old English, "Castle hill")*.

☐ **BURGESS** *(English, "From the town")*.

☐ **BURKE** *(Old French, "Fortress dweller")*.
BERK, BERKE, BOURKE.

☐ **BURL** *(Old English, "Cup bearer")*.

☐ **BURNARD** See BERNARD.

☐ **BURNELL** *(Old French, "Little brown-haired one")*.

☐ **BURNETT** *(English, "Dark skinned")*.

☐ **BURTON** *(Old English, "Fortified town")*.
BERT, BURT, BERTON.

☐ **BYRON** *(English, "From the cottage")*.
BIRON.

C

Most Popular "C" Name.......
CHRISTOPHER

☐ **CAL** Short for names beginning with "Cal".

☐ **CALDER** *(Celtic, "The stony brook")*.

☐ **CALDWELL** *(Old English, "The cold well")*.

☐ **CALEB** *(Hebrew, "Bold," "Dog")*.
Symbolizes affection and fidelity.
CAL, CALE Hebrew: KALEB.

☐ **CALHOUN** *(Irish-Gaelic, "A warrior")*.

☐ **CALVIN** *(Latin, "Bald")*. From John Calvin the 16th century French theologian and leader of the Protestant Reformation.
CAL French: CAUVIN; Italian/ Spanish: CALVINO.

☐ **CAMDEN** *(Scotch, "The winding valley")*.

☐ **CAMERON** *(Scotch, "Crooked nose")*.
CAM.

☐ **CAREY** *(Old Welsh, "From the castle")*.
CARY.

49

☐ **CARL** *(Old German, Karl, "Farmer")*. See CHARLES, KARL.

☐ **CARLETON** *(Old English, "Farmer's town")*
CARL, CHARLTON.

☐ **CARLIN** *(Gaelic-Irish, "Little champion")*.
CARL, CARLING, CARLY.

☐ **CARMINE** *(Latin, "Song")*.

☐ **CARNEY** *(Irish-Gaelic, "Conquering fighter")*.
CARNY (See KEARNEY).

☐ **CAROL** See CHARLES.

☐ **CARROLL** *(Irish, "Champion")*.
CARY (See CHARLES).

☐ **CARSON** *(Welsh, "Son of the marsh dweller")*.

☐ **CARTER** *(Old English, "Driver or maker of carts")*.

☐ **CARY** See CAREY, CARROLL, CHARLES.

☐ **CASEY** *(Irish, "Brave, watchful")*.

☐ **CASPAR** *(Persian, "Keeper of the treasury")*.
CASS, CASPER, JASPER, GASPAR.

☐ **CASS** See CASIMIR, CASPAR, CASSIDY, CASSIUS.

☐ **CASSIDY** *(Irish, "Ingenious")*.
CASS.

☐ **CASSIUS** *(Latin, "Liberator")*.
CASH, CASS, CAZ.

☐ **CECIL** *(Latin, "Blind")*.
Italian: CECILIO; Irish: KILIAN.

☐ **CEDRIC** *(Old English, "Chieftain")*.

☐ **CHAD** *(Celtic, "Defender")*. Also, a short form of Chadwick.

☐ **CHADWICK** *(Old English, "Defenders town")*.

☐ **CHALMERS** *(Gaelic, "Son of the chamberlain")*. See CHAMBERLAIN.

☐ **CHAMBERLAIN** *(Old English, "Keeper of the house")*.
CHALMER, CHAMLERS, CHAMBERLIN.

☐ **CHANCE** *(English, "Fortunate")*. See CHAUNCEY.

☐ **CHANDLER** *(Old French, "Candle maker")*.

☐ **CHAPIN** *(Old French, "Chaplain")*.
CHAPLIN.

☐ **CHAPMAN** *(Old English, "A merchant")*.

50

☐ **CHARLES** *(Old German, "Strong," "Manly")*. Emperor Charles the Great, better known as Charlemagne (742-814).
CARL, CAROL, CARY, CARYL, CARROLL, CHARLEY, CHARLIE, CHIC, CHICK, CHUCK French: CHARLOT; Italian: CARLINO, CARLO; Spanish: CARLOS; Danish: KARL; Dutch: CAREL, KAREL; Danish/German/Swedish: KARL; Slavic: KAROL.

☐ **CHARLTON** See CARLETON.

☐ **CHAUNCEY** *(Old English, "Chancellor")*.
CHANCE, CHAUNCE.

☐ **CHESTER** *(Old English, "From the protected army camp")*. Chester A. Arthur, 21st President of the U.S.
CHESTER, CHESTON, CHET.

☐ **CHET.** See CHESTER.

☐ **CHEVY** *(French, "Chevalier," "knight")*.
CHEV.

☐ **CHRISTIAN** *(Greek, "One who believes in Christ")*.
CHRIS, CHRISSY, CHRISTY, KIT, KRIS French: CHRETIEN; Italian/Spanish: CHRISTIANO; Dutch: KERSTAN; Swedish: KRISTIAN; Slavic: KARSTEN; Scotch: CHRISTIE; Greek, CHRISTIANOS.

☐ **CHRISTOPHER** *(Greek, "Bearing the Christ")*. St. Christopher, 3rd century martyr is the patron saint of travelers.
CHRIS, CHRISSY, CHRISTIE, KIT, KRIS French: CHRISTOPHE; Italian: CHRISTOFORO; Spanish: CRISTOBAL; German: CHRISTOPH, CHRISTOPHORUS, KRISS, STOFFEL; Swedish: KRISTOFER; Polish: KHRISTOF; Russian: CHRISTOF, CHRISTOFER; Greek: CHRISTOPHORUS.

☐ **CHUCK** See CHARLES.

☐ **CLARENCE** *(Latin, "Bright," "Famous")*. Clarence Darrow, attorney.
CLAIR, CLARE.

☐ **CLARK** *(Old French, "A learned man")*. At one time, the word clerk, still pronounced "Clark" in England, meant either a priest (cleric) or a scholar.

☐ **CLAUDE** *(Latin, "Lame")*. Famous for two Roman Emperors named Claudius.
CLAUD, CLAUDIUS Italian: CLAUDIO.

☐ **CLAUS** See NICHOLAS.

☐ **CLAYBORNE** *(Old English, "Born of clay")*.
CLAIBORN, CLAY.

☐ **CLAYTON** *(Old English, "From the clay town")*.
CLAY.

☐ **CLEMENT** *(Latin, "Merciful," "Clemency")*. A disciple of Saint Paul/ St. Clemens is the patron saint of sailors/ Six popes have been named Clement.
CLEM, CLEMENCE, CLEMENS, CLEMMY, CLIM French: **CLEMENT**; Italian/Spanish: **CLEMENTE**; Danish: **KLEMENT**; German: **KLEMENS, MENZ**; Russian: **KLEMET**.

☐ **CLEON** *(Greek, "Famous")*.

☐ **CLEVELAND** *(Old English, "Of the cliff land")*. Cleveland Amory, American author.
CLEVE (See **CLIVE**).

☐ **CLIFF** *(Old English, "Of the cliff")*.

☐ **CLIFFORD** *(Old English, "Of the cliff ford")*. Clifford Odets, playwright.
CLIFF.

☐ **CLIFTON** *(Old English, "From the cliff town")*.
CLIFF.

☐ **CLINTON** *(Old German, "Hill town")*.
CLINT.

☐ **CLIVE** *(Old English, "From the cliff")*.
CLEVE, CLYVE.

☐ **CLYDE** *(Welsh, "Heard from afar")*. The Clyde is a famous river in Scotland. Clyde Cessna, aircraft builder. Clyde Beatty, animal trainer.
CLY.

☐ **CODY** *(Irish, "Helper," "Assistant")*.

☐ **COLE** *(Latin, "The dove")*. "Old King Cole" was an early Welsh ruler. Cole Porter, American composer. (See **COLEMAN, COLAN, COLAS, COLBY, COLIN, COLUMBUS, NICHOLAS**).

☐ **COLBY** *(Old English, "From the coal farm")*.
COLE.

☐ **COLEMAN** *(Old English, "Charcoal vendor")*.
COLE.

☐ **COLIN** *(Irish, "A young animal")*.
COLE. (See **NICHOLAS**).

☐ **CONAN** *(Irish, "Exalted chief")*.
CON, CONAL, CONANT, CONN Irish: **QUINN**.

☐ **CONLAN** *(Irish, "Hero")*.
CON, CONLIN.

☐ **CONNOR** *(Celtic, "Wise")*.

☐ **CONRAD** *(Old German, "Wise counselor")*. Konrad Adenauer, German Chancellor.
CON, CONNIE French: **CONRADE**; Italian: **CONRADO**; Danish: **CORT**; German: **KONRAD, KURT**.

☐ **CONROY** *(Irish, "Wise king")*. CON, CONNIE.

☐ **CONSTANTINE** *(Latin, "Firm," "Constant")*. The first Christian Emperor of Rome, Constantine granted citizenship to the Christians in 313 A.D./ King Constantine of Greece. CON, CONNIE Italian/Spanish: **CONSTANTINO**; German: **CONSTANS, CONSTANTIN, KNOSTANTIN**; Russian: **KONSTANTINE.**

☐ **CONWAY** *(Irish, "The way of wisdom")*. CON, CONNIE.

☐ **COREY** *(Scotch, "Ravine")*. CORY.

☐ **CORNELIUS** *(Latin, "The cornel tree")*. Cornelius Vanderbilt, American Industrialist/ Cornelius McGillicuddy (Connie Mack), baseball manager. CONNIE, CONNY, CORNELL, CORY, NEELEY Spanish: **CORNELIO**; Irish: **CORNEY.**

☐ **CORNELL** *(Old French, "Horn colored")*.

☐ **CORT** *(Old Norse, "Short;" Spanish, "A court;" Old German, "Bold."* See **CONRAD, COURTNEY.**

☐ **CORWIN** *(Latin, "The heart's friend")*.

☐ **COSMO** *(Greek, Kosmos, "Order," "Harmony;" "The universe")*. St. Cosmos is the patron saint of doctors. French: **COSME**; Italian: **COSIMO**; Greek: **KOSMOS.**

☐ **COURTNEY** *(Old French, "From the court")*. CORT.

☐ **CRAIG** *(Scotch, "From the crag or stony hill")*.

☐ **CRANDELL** *(Old English, "From the crane's valley")*. CRAN, CRANDALL.

☐ **CRAWFORD** *(Old English, "From the crow's crossing")*.

☐ **CRISPIN** *(Latin, "Curly haired")*. St. Crispin is the patron saint of shoemakers. CRES, CRESPEN, CRISPIAN French: **CREPET, CREPIN**; Italian: **CRISPINO.**

☐ **CROFTON** *(Old English, "From the pasture land")*. CROFT.

☐ **CROMWELL** *(Old English, "From the winding well")*.

☐ **CROSBY** *(Old English, "From the crossroad")*.

☐ **CULLEN** *(Irish, "Handsome")*. CULL, CULLAN, CULLY.

□ **CURTIS** *(Old French, "The courteous")*.
CURT (See COURTNEY).

□ **CUTLER** *(Old English, "Knifemaker")*.

□ **CY** Short form of names beginning with "Cy".

□ **CYRANO** *(Latin, "Warrior")*. Cyrene was the ancient capital of Africa.

□ **CYRIL** *(Greek, "Lord")*. The 9th century St. Cyril invented the alphabet now used in Russia.
CY, CYR, KYRIL French: CYRILLE; Italian: CIRILLO; Spanish: CIRILO; German: CYRILL; Russian: CIRIL, CIRO; Greek: KYRILLOS.

□ **CYRUS** *(Persian, "The sun")*. In the 5th century Cyrus the Great founded the Persian Empire.
CY Spanish: CIRO; Greek: KYROS.

Most Popular "D" Name...
DAVID

□ **DALE** *(Old English, "The valley")*.

□ **DALLAS** *(Scotch, "The skilled")*. George Dallas, a U.S. vice president, gave his name to Dallas, Texas.

□ **DALTON** *(Old English, "From the valley place")*. Dalton Trumbo, novelist.

□ **DAMON** *(Greek, "Constant one")*. Damon Runyon, American writer. French: DAMIEN; Italian: DAMIANO; German: DAMIAN.

□ **DAN** *(Hebrew, "A judge")*. See DANIEL.

□ **DANA** *(Scandinavian, "From Denmark")*.
DANE.

□ **DANIEL** *(Hebrew, "God is my judge")*. The Biblical prophet who read the writing on the wall and was rescued from the lion's den.
DAN, DANNY Dutch: DANE.

□ **DARCY** *(Old French, "From the ark")*.

□ **DARNELL** *(Old English, "A hidden place")*.

□ **DARRELL** *(Old French, "Darling")*.
DARE, DARREL, DARRYL, DARYL.

□ **DARRENN** *(Irish, "Great one")*.
DARE, DAREN, DARRIN.

□ **DARWIN** *(Anglo-Saxon, "Daring friend")*.

□ **DAVID** *(Hebrew, "Beloved")*. David slew Goliath and became the king of Israel/Saint David the sixth century patron saint of Wales.

DAVE, DAVEY, DAVIE French: **DA-VIDE**; Welsh: **DEVI, DEWEY, DEWI, TAFFY, TAVID**; Russian: **DAVEED**; Hebrew: **DOV**.

☐ **DAVIS** *(Old English, "David's son")*.

☐ **DEAN** *(Old English, "From the valley")*.
DINO.

☐ **DELBERT** *(Old English, "Day-bright")*.
BERT, DALBERT, DEL.

☐ **DELLING** *(Old Norse, "One who shines brightly")*.

☐ **DELMER** *(Old French, "Of the sea")*.
DELMAR.

☐ **DELMORE** *(Old French, "At a marsh")*.
DELM, DELMER.

☐ **DELWIN** *(Old English, "Valley friend")*.
DEL.

☐ **DEMETRIUS** *(Greek, "Of Demeter the earth mother")*. Demeter was the Greek goddess of the harvest and of fertility.
DIMITRY French: **DEMETRE**; Italian: **DEMETRIO**; Russian: **DIMITRI**; Greek: **DEMETRIOS**.

☐ **DENNIS** *(Greek, "Dionysus")*. Dionysus was the Greek god of wine/ St. Denis is patron saint of France.
DEN, DENNEY, DENNY, DION French: **DENYS, DIONE**; Spanish: **DIONIS, DIONISIO**; German: **DIONYS**; Irish: **DENIS**.

☐ **DENTON** *(Old English, "From the valley town")*.
DEN, DENNY, DENT.

☐ **DENVER** *(Old English, "The valley's edge")*.

☐ **DEREK** See DERRICK.

☐ **DERRICK** *(Old German, "Ruler")*.
DEREK, DIRK.

☐ **DESMOND** *(Irish, "Man of the world")*.
DES.

☐ **DEVIN** *(Celtic, "Poet")*.
DEVINE.

☐ **DEVLIN** *(Irish, "Fierce")*.

☐ **DEXTER** *(Latin, "On the right")*.

☐ **DILLON** *(Irish, "Faithful")*.

☐ **DINO** See DEAN.

☐ **DIRK** See DERRICK.

☐ **DIXON** *(Old German, "Son of Richard")*. See **RICHARD**.

☐ **DOLAN** *(Irish, "Black haired")*.

☐ **DOLPH** See ADOLPH.

☐ **DOM** *(Latin, "Master")*.

☐ **DOMINGO** See DOMINIC.

☐ **DOMINIC** *(Latin, "Belonging to the Lord")*. Originally given to boys born on Sunday/ The Spanish Saint Dominic founded the Dominical Order in the 13th century.
DOM, NICK French: **DOMINIQUE**; Italian: **DOMENICO, MENICO**; Spanish: **DOMINGO**; Slavic: **DINKO, DOMINIK**.

☐ **DONAHUE** *(Irish, "Brown chief")*.
DON.

☐ **DONALD** *(Scotch, "World ruler")*. King Donald was Scotland's first Christian King.
DON, DONAL, DONNY Celtic: **DONNALLY, DONNELL**.

☐ **DONNELLY** *(Irish, "Dark man")*.
DON, DONNIE.

☐ **DONOVAN** *(Irish, "Dark warrior")*.
DON, DONNIE.

☐ **DORE** see DORIAN.

☐ **DORIAN** *(Greek, "A Dorian")*. The Dorians were the 11th century B.C. settlers of Greece.
DORE, DORY Greek: **DORUS**.

☐ **DORY** *(French, "Golden haired")*.

☒ **DOUGLAS** *(Scotch, "Dark water")*. The Douglas clan was famous in Scottish history.
DOUG, DOUGIE, DUGAL, DUGALD, DUGAN.

☐ **DOYLE** *(Irish, "Dark stranger")*. Derives from the Scotch Douglas clan.
DUGAL Celtic: **DUGALD, DUGAN**.

☐ **DRAKE** *(Middle English, "Male duck or swan")*.

☐ **DREW** *(Old German, "Trustworthy")*.

☐ **DUANE** *(Irish, "Dark complected")*.
DWAYNE.

☐ **DUDLEY** *(Old English, "From the people's meadow")*.

☐ **DUKE** *(Latin, "Leader")*.

☐ **DUNCAN** *(Scotch, "Brown chief or warrior")*. Duncan, 11th century king of Scotland, was murdered by Macbeth.
DUN.

☐ **DUSTIN** *(Old German, "Brave fighter")*.
DUSTY.

☐ **DWAYNE** See DUANE.

☐ **DWIGHT** *(Old German, "White," "Fair")*.

□ **DYLAN** *(Welsh, "Son of the wave")*. Dylan was the Welsh god of the sea.

□ **EARL** *(Old English, "Nobleman")*. EARLY Celtic: **ERROL**.

□ **EATON** *(Old English, "From the river estate")*.

□ **EBENEZER** *(Hebrew, "The stone of help")*. Ebenezer was the name of the stone placed by Samuel to commemorate the defeat of the Philistines.
EB, EBBIE, EBEN.

□ **EBERHARD** *(Old German, "Strong as a boar")*. See **EVERARD**.

□ **ED** The short form of names beginning with "Ed".

□ **EDAN** *(Irish, "Fire")*.

□ **EDGAR** *(Old English, "Rich spear")*.
ED, EDDIE, NED French: **EDGARD**; Italian: **EDGARDO**.

□ **EDISON** *(Old English, "Son of Edward")*.
ED, EDDY.

□ **EDMUND** *(Old English, "Defender of property")*. St. Edmond was the 9th century king of England/ Eamonde Valera was president of Ireland.
ED, EDDIE, EDMONT, NED French: **EDMOND**; Italian: **EDMONDO**; Spanish: **EDMUNDO**; Irish: **EAMON**.

□ **EDWARD** *(Old English, "Protector of the rich")*. Eight kings of England were named Edward; the term Edwardian describes this period in English history.
ED, EDDY, NED, TED, TEDDY French: **EDOUARD**; Italian/Spanish: **EDUARDO**; German: **EDUARD**; Swedish: **EDVARD**.

□ **ELDWIN** *(Old English, "Rich friend")*.
ED, EDDIE Italian/Spanish: **EDUINO**.

□ **EGAN** *(Irish, "Ardent")*.

□ **ELDON** *(Old English, "Alder hill")*.

□ **ELDRIDGE** See **ALDRICH**.

□ **ELEAZAR** *(Hebrew, "God hath helped")*. The biblical Eleazar was the son of Aaron.
ELEAZER, ELIEZER, ELY, LAZAR, LAZARUS Hebrew: **ELAZAR**.

□ **ELI** *(Hebrew, "The highest")*. The biblical priest who trained Samuel/

St. Eloi is the patron saint of gold-smiths.
ELY.

☐ **ELIJAH** *(Hebrew, "Jehovah is God")*. Also known as Elias, Elijah was a prominent Hebrew prophet.
ELI, ELIAS, ELIOT, ELLIOT, ELLIS French: **ELIE**; Italian: **ELIA**; German: **ELIA, ELIAS**; Hebrew: **ELIAS, ELIHU.**

☐ **ELLERY** *(Middle English, "From the alder trees island")*.
ELLARY.

☐ **ELLIOT** See **ELIJAH.**

☐ **ELLIS** See **ELIJAH.**

☐ **ELLISON** *(Old English, "Son of Ellis")*.

☐ **ELLSWORTH** *(Old English, "Nobleman's estate")*.

☐ **ELMER** *(Old English, "Noble and famous")*. See **ALYMET.**

☐ **ELMO** *(Italian, "Amiable")*. St. Elmo is the patron saint of seamen.

☐ **ELMORE** *(Old English, "Elm-tree moor")*.

☐ **ELROY** *(Old French, "Royal")*. See **LEROY.**

☐ **ELTON** *(Old English, "The old town")*.

☐ **ELVIN** See **ELWIN.**

☐ **ELVIS** *(Scandinavian, "All-wise")*. See **ALVIS.**

☐ **ELWIN** *(Old English, "Elf friend")*.
ELVIN.

☐ **ELWOOD** *(Old English, "From the old woods")*.
WOODY.

☐ **EMANUAL** See **EMMANUEL.**

☐ **EMERY, EMMERY, EMORY** *(Old German, "Joint ruler")*.
EMERSON French: **EMERI**; German: **EMMERICH.**

☐ **EMIL** *(Latin, "The industrious")*. French: **EMILE**; Italian/Spanish: **EMILO**; Welsh: **EMLYN.**

☐ **EMMANUEL** *(Hebrew, "God is in us")*. A 15th century Portuguese king.
IMMANUEL, MANNIE, MANNY Italian: **EMMANUELE**; Spanish: **MANUEL**; German: **EMANUEL.**

☐ **EMMETT** *(Old English, "Industrious")*. Robert Emmett, Irish patriot.

☐ **EMORY** See **EMERY.**

☐ **ENGELBERT** *(Old German, "Bright angel")*.
INGLEBERT.

☐ **ENOCH** *(Hebrew, "The dedicated")*. The Biblical Enoch was a patriarch and the father of Methuselah.

☐ **ENOS** *(Hebrew, "Man").*

☐ **EPHRAIM** *(Hebrew, "Very fruitful").* In the Bible Ephraim was the second son of Joseph and founder of the tribe of Ephraim.
EFREM, EPHRIM Russian: EPHREM; Hebrew: EPHRAYIM.

☐ **ERASMUS** *(Greek, "Worthy of love").* St. Erasmus is the patron saint of sailors.
Italian/Spanish: ERASMO; Greek: ERASMIOS.

☐ **ERIC** *(Scandinavian, "Ruler").* A Viking hero, Eric the Red was father of Leif Ericson.
RICK, RICKY German: ERICH; Scandinavian: ERIK.

☐ **ERLAND** *(Old English, "Nobleman's land").*

☐ **ERNEST** *(Old English, "Intent," "sincere").*
ERNIE, ERNY Italian/Spanish: ERNESTO; German: ERNST.

☐ **ERROL** See EARL.

☐ **ERSKINE** *(Scotch, "High cliff").*

☐ **ERWIN** *(Old English, "Sea friend").* See IRVING.

☐ **ESAU** *(Hebrew, "Covered with hair").*

☐ **ETHAN** *(Hebrew, "Firmness").* Ethan Allen, head of the Green Mountain Boys in the American Revolution.

☐ **EUGENE** *(Greek, "Noble").* Four popes were named Eugene/ Prince Eugene of Austria led the Crusades against the Turks.
GENE Italian/Spanish: EUGENIO; German: EUGEN.

☐ **EVAN** *(Welsh, "A youth").*
EVIN, EWAN, OWEN.

☐ **EVERETT** See EBERHARD, EVERARD.

☐ **EVERLEY** *(Old English, "From Ever's meadow").*

☐ **EZEKIAL** *(Hebrew, "God strengthens").* One of the biblical Hebrew prophets.
EZEKIAH, ZEKE French/German: EZECHIEL; Spanish: EZEQUIEL.

☐ **EZRA** *(Hebrew, "Helper").* Ezra led the Israelites back to Jerusalem from captivity.
French: ESDRAS; German: ESRA; Greek, ESDRAS.

F Most Popular "F" Name.... **FREDERICK**

☐ **FABIAN** *(Latin, "Bean grower").* The Roman general Fabius Maximus defeated Hannibal by use of delaying

tactics/ St. Fabian was the Bishop of Rome.
French: **FABIEN**; Italian: **FABIO**.

☐ **FARLEY** *(Old English, "Fair meadow")*.

☐ **FARRELL** *(Irish, "The valorous")*.
FARREL.

☐ **FELIX** *(Latin, "Happy," "Prosperous")*. The name of four popes and many saints.
Italian: **FELICE**; Portuguese: **FELIZ**.

☐ **FENTON** *(Old English, "From the town near the fen or marsh")*.

☐ **FERDINAND** *(Old German, "Bold peace")*. The name of Spanish and Portuguese kings/ Fernando Magellan was the first person to sail around the world.
FERDIE, FERDY Italian: FERDINANDO, FERRANDO; Spanish: FERNANDO, HERNANDO.

☐ **FERGUS** *(Irish, "The choice")*.
FERGIE.

☐ **FERRAND** *(Old French, "Gray hair")*.

☐ **FERRIS** See PETER.

☐ **FILBERT** *(Old English, "Brilliant one")*.
PHIL, PHILBERT.

☐ **FILMORE** *(Old English, "Highly remarkable")*.

☐ **FINLEY** *(Irish, "Fair-haired soldier")*.
FINDLEY, FINLAY.

☐ **FINN** *(Irish, "Fair-haired")*. Finn MacCool was Ireland's famous 2nd Century hero/ Saint Finnian was an Irish saint.
FINNY.

☐ **FITZ** *(Latin/French, "Son")*.

☐ **FITZGERALD** *(Old English, "Son of Gerald")*. See **GERALD**.

☐ **FITZPATRICK** *(Old English, "Son of the noble person")*. See **PATRICK**.

☐ **FLEMING** *(English, "From Flanders")*.

☐ **FLETCHER** *(Middle English, "Maker of arrows")*.

☐ **FLOYD** See LLOYD.

☐ **FLYNN** *(Irish, "Son of the red-haired man")*.

☐ **FORD** *(Old English, "A river crossing")*.

☐ **FORREST** *(Old French, "Of the forest")*.
FOREST, FORESTER, FORRESTER, FORSTER, FOSTER.

60

☐ **FOSTER** See FORREST.

☐ **FOWLER** *(Old English, "Hunter of fowl").*

☐ **FRANCIS** *(Latin, "Frenchman").* Three saints were named Francis/ The first Saint Francis of Assisi is the patron saint of birds.
FRAN, FRANK, FRANKIE, FRANKY
French: FRANCHOT, FRANCOIS;
Italian: FRANCESCO, FRANCO;
Spanish: FRANCISCO, PANCHO;
German: FRANC, FRANCK, FRANZ;
Dutch: FRANS.

☐ **FRANK** See FRANKLIN, FRANCIS.

☐ **FRANKLIN** *(Old German, "A free man").*
FRANK, FRANKIE, FRANKY.

☐ **FRANZ** See FRANCIS.

☐ **FRAZER** *(Old French, "Strawberry").*
FRASIER.

☐ **FREDERICK** *(Old German, "Powerful and Peaceful").* The name of great German emperors/ Frederic I created the German Empire.
FRED, FREDDIE, FREDDY, FREDRIC
French: FREDERIC; Italian: FEDERIGO; Spanish: FEDERICO; German: FRIEDEL, FRIEDRICH, FRITZ; Swedish: FREDRIK.

☐ **FREEMAN** *(Old English, "Free man").*

☐ **FREMONT** *(Old German, "Protector of freedom").*

☐ **FRITZ** See FREDERICK.

☐ **FULLER** *(Old English, "A man who worked with cloth").*

☐ **FULTON** *(Old English, "Field town").*

G Most Popular "G" Name. . . **GREGORY**

☐ **GABRIEL** *(Hebrew, "Man of God").* The Archangel of the Annunciation.
GABE Italian/Spanish: GABRIELLO; Russian: GAVRIL.

☐ **GALE** *(Irish, "Stranger"/Old English, "Gay," "Lively").*
GAIL, GAYLE.

☐ **GALEN** *(Greek, "Sea calm").* The great 2nd century physician.

☐ **GALLAGHER** *(Irish, "Eager helper").*

☐ **GARDENER** *(English, "A gardener").*
GARD, GARDINER, GARDNER, GERTH.

61

□ **GARFIELD** *(Old English, "War field")*.

□ **GARNER** *(Old French, "Guardian")*.

□ **GARNETT** *(Old English, "Spear-warrior"/Latin, "A seed")*.

□ **GARRETT** *(Old English, "Powerful with the spear")*.
GAR, GARET, GARETT, JARETT Scandinavian: GARTH; Welsh: GARETH.

□ **GARRICK** *(Old English, "Spear-king")*.

□ **GARSON** *(Old English, "Son of Gar, warrior")*.

□ **GARTH** *(Old Norse, "Gardener")*. See GARRETT.

□ **GARVEY** *(Old English, "Spear bearer")*.
GAR

□ **GARVIN** *(Old English, "Spear friend")*.
GAR, GARWIN.

□ **GARY** *(Old German, "Spear carrier")*. See GERALD.

□ **GASTON** *(French, "A native of Gascony in France")*.

□ **GAVIN** *(Old Welsh, "Hawk of Battle")*. In Arthurian legend, Sir Gawain was the nephew of King Arthur.
GAVEN, GAWAIN.

□ **GAYLORD** *(Old French, "Lively one")*.
GAY.

□ **GAYNOR** *(Gaelic, "Son of the fair-headed one")*.

□ **GENE** See EUGENE.

□ **GEOFFREY** See JEFFREY.

□ **GEORGE** *(Greek, "A farmer")*. St. George is the patron saint of England/Kings named George ruled England for 116 straight years/The English flag is the banner of St. George.
GEORGIE, GEORGY French: GEORGES, GEORGET; Italian: GIORGIO; Spanish: JORGE; Danish: GEORG, JOREN; Dutch, JORIS; Swedish: GORAN; Swiss: JORG; Russian: IGOR; Scotch: GEORDIE.

□ **GERALD** *(Old German, "Spear-rule")*.
GERALD, JERALD, JEROLD, JERROLD, JERRIE, JERRY French: GERALDE, GERAUD, GIRAUD, GIRAULD; Italian/Spanish: GERARDO, GIRALDO; German: GEROLD.

□ **GERARD** *(Old German, "Spear hard")*.
GARRARD, GERRIE, GERRY, JER-

RARD, JERRY Italian/Spanish: GER-ARDO; German: GERHARD.

☐ **GERSHOM** *(Hebrew, "The exile")*.

☐ **GIBSON** *(Old English, "Son of Gilbert")*. See GILBERT.

☐ **GIDEON** *(Hebrew, "The hewer", "Feller of trees")*. Gideon freed the Israelites and ruled Israel for 40 years.

☐ **GIFFORD** *(Old English, "Gift-strong")*.
GIFF.

☐ **GILBERT** *(Germanic/French, "Bright pledge")*. Wilbert and Gilbert are the same names, though the French use a "g" sound instead of a "w".
BERT, BERTY, BURT, GIB, GIBB, GIL, GILBURT French: GUILBERT; Italian: GILBERTO; German: WILBERT, WILBUR.

☐ **GILBY** *(Irish, "Yellow hair")*.

☐ **GILES** *(Latin, "Shield-bearer" /Greek, "Youthful")*. St. Giles is the patron saint of Edinburgh.
French: GILLES; Spanish: GIL.

☐ **GILLIAN** *(Celtic, "Servant of a chieftain")*.
GILL, GILLY.

☐ **GILROY** *(Irish, "Servant of the king")*.
GIL.

☐ **GLADE** *(Old English, "Sunny one")*.

☐ **GLADWIN** *(Old English, "Cheerful friend")*.

☐ **GLEN** *(Irish, "Valley")*.
GLYN.

☐ **GLENDON** *(Scotch/Gaelic "The fortress in the den")*.

☐ **GODFREY** See JEFFREY.

☐ **GODWIN** *(Old English, "Friend of God")*.
GOODWIN.

☐ **GORDON** *(Old English, "Round hill")*.
GORDIE, GORDY.

☐ **GRADY** *(Irish, "Noble")*.

☐ **GRAHAM** *(Old English, "From the gray home")*.

☒ **GRANT** *(Middle English, "Grand")*.

☐ **GRAYSON** *(Old English, "Son of the bailiff")*.

☐ **GREELEY** *(Old English, "From the pleasant meadow")*.

☒ **GREGORY** *(Greek, "Watchful")*. Sixteen popes were named Gregory, including Gregory the Great who established the Gregorian calendar.
GREG, GREGG French: GREGOIRE;

Italian/Spanish: **GREGORIO**; German: **GREGOR**; Greek: **GREGORIOS**.

☐ **GRIFFIN** *(Latin, A mythical animal with the body of a lion and the head and wings of an eagle)*. **GRIFF**.

☐ **GROVER** *(Old English, "Gardener")*.

☐ **GUNTHER** *(Old Norse, "Warrior")*. **GUNNAR, GUNTER**.

☐ **GUSTAVUS** *(Swedish, "Staff of the Goths")*. **GUS** French/German: **GUSTAV**; Italian/Spanish: **GUSTAVO**; Swedish: **GOSTA, GUSTAF**.

☐ **GUY** *(Old French, "Guide")*. **WYATT** Italian/Spanish: **GUIDO**.

Most Popular "**H**" Name...
HOWARD

☐ **HADDEN** *(Old English, "From the heath place")*.

☐ **HADLEY** *(Old English, "From the heath")*. **HEDLEY**.

☐ **HAGEN** *(Irish, "Young")*. **HAGAN**.

☐ **HAL** See HAROLD, HARRY.

☐ **HALDEN** *(Old Norse, "Half Dane")*. **HALDANE, HALDIN**.

☐ **HALE** *(Old English, "Hero")*. **HAL, HALEY**

☐ **HALEY** *(Irish, "Ingenious")*. See **HALE**.

☐ **HALSEY** *(Old English, "Hazel-tree island")*. **HAL**

☐ **HALTON** *(Old English, "Hillside town")*.

☐ **HAMILTON** *(Old English, "From the mountain hamlet")*.

☐ **HAMLIN** *(Old French/German, "Little home-lover")*. Hamlin Garland, U.S. writer. **HAM**.

☐ **HANLEY** *(Old English, "From the high lea")*.

☐ **HANS** See JOHN.

☐ **HANK** See HENRY.

☐ **HARAM** *(Hebrew, "A mountaineer")*.

☐ **HARDEN** *(Old German, "To be brave")*. **HARDY**.

☐ **HARDING** (*Old English, "Brave one's son"*). See HARDEN.

☐ **HARLAN** (*Old English, "Army land"*).
HARLAND, HARLIN.

☐ **HARLEY** (*Old English, "Army meadow"*).
ARLEY.

☐ **HARLOW** (*Old English, "From the fortified hill"*).
ARLO.

☐ **HARMAN** (*Old English, "A deer keeper"*).

☐ **HARMON** (*Greek, "Harmony"*).

☐ **HAROLD** (*Old Norse, "In command of an army"*). Harold was the last of the Saxon kings of England.
HAL, HARRY, HERRICK Italian: ARALDO, AROLDO; Danish: HARALD.

☐ **HARPER** (*Old English, "Harp player"*).

☐ **HARRIS, HARRISON** (*Old English, "Son of Harry"*).

☐ **HARRY** (*Old English, "Soldier"*). See HAROLD, HENRY.

☐ **HARTLEY** (*Old English, "Deer meadow"*).

☐ **HARTMAN** (*Old English, "Deer keeper"*).

☐ **HARVEY** (*Old German, "Army warrior"*).
HARV, HERVEY French: HERVE.

☐ **HASKEL** (*Hebrew, "Understanding"*).

☐ **HAWLEY** (*Old English, "From the hedged meadow"*).

☐ **HAWTHORNE** (*Old English, "The hawthorn plant"*).

☐ **HAYDEN** (*Old English, "From the hedge valley"*).

☐ **HAYES** (*Old English, "From the hedge place"*).

☐ **HAYWARD** (*Old English, "A hedge guard"*).

☐ **HAYWOOD** (*Old English, "From the hedge wood"*).
HEYWOOD.

☐ **HAZAEL** (*Hebrew, "Whom God sees"*).

☐ **HERBERT** (*Old German, "Bright man"*).

☐ **HECTOR** (*Greek, "To hold fast"*). Hector of Troy was the hero of the Trojan War and of Homer's Iliad.
Italian: ETTORE.

☐ **HENRY** (*Old German, "Ruler of the estate"*). Eight English kings and six German emperors bore this name.
HAL, HANK, HARRY, HENRI Italian:

ENRICO, ENZIO; Spanish: **ENRIQUE;**
Danish/Dutch: **HENDRIK;** German:
HEINRICH. HEINTZ; Swedish: **HEN-
RIK.**

☐ **HERB** See HERBERT.

☐ **HERBERT** *(Old German,
"Bright warrior").*
**HARBERT, BERT, HEBERT, HERB,
HERBIE, HERBY** Italian: **ERBERTO;**
Spanish: **HERIBERTO.**

☐ **HERMAN** *(Old German, "The
armed").* Saint Armand is the patron
saint of the Netherlands.
**ARMIN, ERMIN, HARMAN, HARMON,
HERMON, HERMY** French: **ARMAND;**
Italian: **ARMINIO, ERMANNO;** Spanish: **ARMANDO;** German: **HERMANN.**

☐ **HERNE** *(Anglo-Saxon, "Heron").*
HEARNE.

☐ **HERSHEL** *(Hebrew, "Deer").*
HERSCH.

☐ **HEWETT/HEWITT** Diminu-
tive of HUGH; see HUGH.

☐ **HEYWOOD** See HAYWOOD

☐ **HILARY** *(Latin, "Cheerful,
hilarious").* More than a dozen saints
have been named either Hilarius, Hil-
arion, Hilari or Hilarinus.
HILLARY, HILLERY Latin: **HILARI-
US;** French: **HILAIRE;** Italian: **ILIRIO;**
Spanish: **HILARIO;** Russian: **HILAR-
ION;** Welsh: **ILAR;** Greek: **HILARIOS.**

☐ **HILBERT** *(Old German,"Bright
hill").*

☐ **HILDER** *(Old English, "Warrior").*

☐ **HILTON** *(Old English, "The hill
estate").*

☐ **HIRAM** *(Hebrew, "Noble").*
HY, HYRAM.

☐ **HOBART** See HUBERT.

☐ **HOGAN** *(Irish, "Youth").*

☐ **HOLDEN** *(Old English, "From
the hollow in the valley").*

☐ **HOLLIS** *(Old English, "From
the holly grove").*
HOLLEY, HOLLY.

☐ **HOLT** *(Old English, "From the
woods").*

☐ **HOMER** *(Greek, "Pledge").* Hom-
er was the blind poet who wrote the
"Iliad" and "Odyssey" epics.
French: **HOMERE;** Italian: **OMERO;**
Greek: **HOMEROS.**

☐ **HORACE** *(Latin, "Keeper of the
hours").*
HORATIO Spanish: **HORACIO.**

☐ **HORTON** *(Old English, "From
the gray estate").*

☐ **HOUSTON** *(Old English, "Hill-
town").*

☐ **HOWARD** *(Germanic, "Watchman")*.
HOVARD, HOWIE.

☐ **HUBERT** *(Old German, "Bright mind")*. St. Hubert is the patron saint of hunters.
BERT, HOBARD, HOBART, HOYT, HUBBARD, HUBE, HUBIE Italian: UBERTO; Spanish: HUBERTO; German: HUGIBERT.

☐ **HUDSON** *(Old English, "Son of Hyde")*.

☐ **HUGH** *(Old English, "Mind")*.
HEWETT, HUEY, HUGHES, HUGHIE, HUTCH French: HUGUES; Italian: UGO, UGOLINO; German: HUGO.

☐ **HUGO** See HUGH.

☐ **HUMPHREY** *(Old German, "Hun peace")*.
French: ONFROI; Italian: ONFREDO, ONOFREDO; German: HUMFRIED.

☐ **HUNTER** *(Old English, "A hunter")*.
HUNT.

☐ **HUNTINGTON** *(Old English, "Hunting estate")*.
HUNT.

☐ **HUNTLEY** *(Old English, "Hunter's meadow")*.
HUNT.

☐ **HUXLEY** *(Old English, "Hugh's meadow")*.

☐ **HYATT** *(Old English, "High gate")*.
HIATT.

I Most Popular "I" Name. . . .
ISAAC

☐ **IAN** See JOHN.

☐ **ICHABOD** *(Hebrew, "Inglorious")*.

☐ **INGEMAR** *(Scandinavian, "Famous son")*.
INGMAR.

☐ **IMMANUEL** See EMMANUEL.

☐ **INGLEBERT** See ENGELBERT.

☐ **INGRAM** *(Old German, "Angelraven")*.

☐ **INNIS** *(Irish, "From the island")*.
INNES.

☐ **IRA** *(Hebrew, "The watchful")*.

☐ **IRVING** *(Old English, "Sea friend")*.
ERWIN, IRV, IRVIN, IRWIN, (See MARVIN, MERVIN).

☐ **IRWIN** See IRVING.

□ **ISAAC** *(Hebrew, "Laughter").* Isaac was the son of Abraham and Sarah/Saint Isaac is the patron saint of Russia.
IKE Italian: **SACCO**; German: **ISAAK**.

□ **ISAIAH** *(Hebrew, "Salvation of the Lord").* The great prophet of Israel who lived in the 7th century B.C. ISA.

□ **ISIDORE** *(Greek, "Gift of Isis").* IZZY Italian: **ISIDORO**; Spanish: **ISIDRO**; German: **ISIDOR**; Greek: **ISIDOROS**.

□ **IVAN** See JOHN.

□ **IVAR** *(Old Norse, "Archer").* See YVES.

□ **IVES** See YVES.

J

Most Popular "J" Name....
JASON

□ **JACK** See JACOB, JOHN, JACKSON.

□ **JACKSON** *(Old English, "Son of Jack").*
JACK, JACKIE.

□ **JACOB** *(Hebrew, "Supplanter").* Jacob was the biblical son of Abraham/His sons founded the tribes of Israel.
COBB, JACK, JAKE, JAMES, JAMEY, JAY French: **JACQUES**; Italian: **GIACOBO, GIACOPO, GIACOMO**; Spanish: **JAIME, JACOBO, JAYME**; German: **JAKOB**; Irish: **SEAMUS** (See JAMES).

□ **JAIME** See JACOB, JAMES.

□ **JAMES** *(Hebrew, from Jacob, "The supplanter").* St. James is the patron saint (Santiago) of Spain/ There were kings of England, Spain and Scotland named James, including King James I of England who had the Bible translated into English/ Five American presidents have been named James.
JAMEY, JAY, JEM, JEMMY, JIM, JIMMY Italian: **IAGO, GIACOMO**; Spanish: **DIEGO, JAIME**; Portuguese: **JAYME**; Irish: **SEAMUS, SHAMUS**; Scottish: **HAMISH**; Russian: **JASCHA**.

□ **JAN** See JOHN.

□ **JARED** See JORDAN.

□ **JARVIS** *(Old German, "Sharp spear").*
JERVIS French: **GERVAISE, JERVOISE**.

□ **JASON** *(Greek, "The healer").* In Greek mythology he found the Golden

68

Fleece.
JACIE, JAY.

☐ **JASPER** See CASPAR.

☐ **JAY** See JACOB, JAMES, JASON.

☐ **JEAN** See JOHN.

☐ **JEDEDIAH** *(Hebrew, "Loved by the Lord")*.
JED.

☐ **JEFF** See JEFFERSON, JEFFREY.

☐ **JEFFERSON** *(Old English, "Son of Jeffrey")*.
JEFF.

☒ **JEFFREY** *(Old German, "District peace")*. The name was introduced to England as Godfrey with the Norman invasion/Saint Gottfried conquered Jerusalem.
GEOFF, GEOFFREY, GODFREY, JEFF, JEFFY French: GEOFFROI, JEOFFROI; Italian: GIOTTO, GOFFREDO; Spanish: GOFREDO; Dutch: GOVERT; German: GOTTFRIED.

☐ **JERALD** See GERALD.

☐ **JEREMIAH** See JEREMY.

☐ **JEREMY** *(Hebrew, "God is high")*. Jeremiah, the prophet of Judah/Jeremy is an English form of Jeremiah.
JEREMIAH, JERRY French: JERE-MIE; Italian: GEREMIA; Spanish/German: JEREMIAS.

☐ **JEROME** *(Greek, "Sacred name")*.
JERRY Italian: GERONIMO, GIRO-LAMO; Spanish: JEROMO, JERON-IMO; German: HIERONYMUS; Russian: JERONIM; Greek: HIERONY-MOS.

☐ **JERRARD** See GERARD.

☐ **JERRY** See GERALD, JERE-MIAH, JEREMY, JEROME.

☐ **JESSE** *(Hebrew, "Jehovah exists")*. Jesse was the biblical father of David.
JESS, JESSIE, JESSY.

☐ **JESUS** Originally a form of the name Joshua, it is now used as a boy's name only in Latin speaking countries.

☐ **JETHRO** *(Hebrew, "Pre-eminent")*. The father-in-law of Moses.

☐ **JIM** See JAMES.

☐ **JOE** See JOSEPH.

☐ **JOEL** *(Hebrew, "Jehovah is the Lord")*. In the Bible, Joel was a Hebrew prophet.
Hebrew: YOEL.

☐ **JOHN** *(Hebrew, "God is gracious")*. Traditionally this has been the most popular name for boys in its various forms worldwide/There have been 84 saints John, including St. John the Apostle and St. John the Baptist/John Calvin led the Protestant reformation.

JACK, JACKIE, JACKY, JOHAN, JOHNNY, JON, ZANE Latin: **JOANNES, JOHANNES**; French: **JEAN**; Italian: **GIAN, GIANNI, GIANNINI, GIOVANNI, VANNI**; Portuguese: **JOAO**; Spanish: **JUAN, JUANITO**; Bavarian: **HANSEL**; Danish: **JANNE, JENS, JOHAN**; Dutch/Belgian: **JAN**; German: **HANS**; Polish: **JAN, JANEK**; Russian: **IVAN, VANKA**; Irish: **SEAN, SHANE, SHAWN**; Scotch: **IAN, JOCK**; Welsh: **EVAN**; Greek: **GIANNES, JANNES, JOANNES**; Hebrew: **YOHANAN**. See also p. 27.

☐ **JONAH** *(Hebrew, "Dove")*. A biblical prophet.
JONAS.

☐ **JONATHAN** *(Hebrew, "Jehovah given")*. In the Bible, Jonathan was the friend of David and the son of Saul.
JON.

☐ **JORDAN** *(Hebrew, "Descending")*. The descending river Jordan was originally named Jared.
JARED French: **JOURDAIN**; Italian: **GIORDANO.**

☐ **JOSEPH** *(Hebrew, "He shall add")*. Famous for Joseph, the son of Jacob and Joseph the husband of Mary.
JO, JOE, JOEY Latin: **JOSEPHUS**; French: **JOSEPHE**; Italian: **GIUSEPPE**; Spanish: **JOSE**; Russian: **JOSEEF, OSEEP**; Arabic: **YUSEF, YUSSUF**; Greek: **IOSEPH**; Hebrew: **YOSEPH.**

☐ **JOSHUA** *(Hebrew, "Jehovah saves")*. A form of Jehoshea, the name revealed by God to Moses never to be pronounced/Joshua led the children of Israel to the promised land/Jesus is the Greek form of this name.
JOSH French: **JOSUE**; German: **JOSUA**; Hebrew: **YEHOSHA.**

☐ **JUDAH** *(Hebrew, "Praise")*. The biblical son of Jacob, who founded one of the tribes of Israel and restored the kingdom of Judea/St. Jude was one of the twelve apostles also known as Thaddeus.
JUD, JUDD, JUDA, JUDAH, JUDAS, JUDE.

☐ **JULIAN** *(Latin, "Belonging to Julius")*. There have been many saints Julian/One is the patron saint of travelers.
JULES French: **JULIEN**; Italian: **GIULIANO**; Danish: **JULIANUS**; German: **JULIAN, JULIANUS.**

☐ **JUSTIN** *(Latin, "The just").* Justinian I was a Byzantine emperor who conquered Rome.
JOS, JUS, JUSTUS French: **JUSTE**; Italian: **GIUSTINO, GIUSTO**; Spanish: **JUSTINO, JUSTO**; German: **JUST, JUSTUS**.

K

Most Popular "K" Name...
KEVIN

☐ **KANE** *(Celtic, "Tribute," or "Little warlike one").*

☐ **KARL** See **CHARLES**.

☐ **KAROL** See **CHARLES**.

☐ **KASPER** See **CASPAR**.

☐ **KEANE** *(Old English, "Bold, sharp").*

☐ **KEARNEY** *(Celtic, "Foot soldier").* See **CARNEY**.

☐ **KEENAN** *(Irish, "Ancient one").*

☐ **KEIR** See **KERR**.

☐ **KEITH** *(Scotch, "Enclosed place").*

☐ **KELLER** *(Irish, "Little friend").*

☐ **KELLY** *(Irish, "Warrior").*

☐ **KELSEY** *(Old Norse, "One from the ship island").*

☐ **KELVIN** *(Irish, "Warrior friend").* **KELWIN**.

☐ **KEN** *(Scotch, "A chief").* See **KENNETH**, other names beginning with "Ken".
KENNY, KENT.

☐ **KENDALL** *(Old English, "Chief of the dale").*
KEN, KENDAL, KENDELL, KENNY.

☐ **KENDRICK** *(Irish, "Royal king").*
KEN, KENNY.

☐ **KENNEDY** *(Irish, "Helmeted head").*

☐ **KENNETH** *(Scotch, "Handsome").* The first King of Scotland was Kenneth/The Scotch St. Kennet is the patron saint of Kilkenny, Ireland.
KEN, KENNET, KENNY.

☐ **KENRICK** *(Old English, "Royal ruler").*

☐ **KENT** *(Welsh, "Radiant").*
KEN, KENNY.

☐ **KENTON** *(Old English, "The chief's headquarters").*

☐ **KENYON** *(Irish, "White headed").*
KEN, KENNY.

☐ **KERMIT** *(Irish, "Free man").* **KER**.

☐ **KERRY** *(Irish, "Dark haired")*.

☐ **KERWIN** *(Irish, "Dark one")*.
KIRWIN.

☑ **KEVIN** *(Irish, "Gentle and loved")*. St. Kevin is one of the patron saints of Dublin.

☐ **KILLIAN** *(Irish, "Little warlike one")*.

☐ **KIM** *(Old English, "Chief")*.

☐ **KIMBALL** *(Old Welsh, "Warrior chief")*.

☐ **KIP** *(Old English, "From the pointed hill")*.
KIPP.

☐ **KIRBY** *(Old Norse, "From the church town")*.
KERBY.

☐ **KIRK** *(Old Norse, "A church")*.

☐ **KIRKWOOD** *(Old English, "The church forest")*.

☐ **KIRWIN** See KERWIN.

☐ **KIT** See CHRISTOPHER.

☐ **KONRAD** See CONRAD.

☐ **KURT** See CONRAD.

☒ **KYLE** *(Irish, "Handsome")*.
KILE.

Most Popular
"L" Name....
LAWRENCE

☐ **LADD** *(Middle English, "Boy", "Attendant")*.
LAD.

☐ **LAMAR** *(Latin, "From the sea"/ Old German, "Famous in the land")*.

☐ **LAMONT** *(Old Norse, "A lawyer")*.
LAMOND.

☐ **LANCE** *(Old French, Lancelot, "One who serves")*. Lancelot was a knight of King Arthur's Round Table.
LANCELOT.

☐ **LANDON** *(Old English, "The long hill")*.
LANGDON.

☐ **LANE** *(Old English, "A country road")*.

☐ **LARS** See LAWRENCE.

☐ **LATHROP** *(Old English, "The storehouse village")*.

☐ **LAUREN** See LAWRENCE.

☐ **LAWRENCE** *(Latin, "The laurel," "Crown of glory")*. The laurel tree was sacred to the ancient Greeks who made the leaves into wreaths for use as a crown of distinction/One of the

72

nine saints of this name was the Irish Saint Lawrence who helped build Saint Patrick's Cathedral in Dublin/ Saint Laurence was a 3rd Century martyr.
LARRY, LARSON, LAURAN, LAUREN, LAURENCE, LAURENT, LAWRY, LAWS, LAWSON, LON, LONNIE, LOREN, LORIN, LORN, LORRY French: **LAURENT**; Italian/Spanish: **LORENZO**; Danish: **LAR, LAURITZ, LORENZ**; German: **LORENZ**; Scandinavian: **LORENS**; Swedish: **LARS, LAURENTIUS**; Swiss: **LENZ, LORI**; Russian: **LAVRENTIJ**; Slavic: **LOVRE**; Irish: **LANTY, LARRY, LAURENCE**; Scottish: **LAWREN**.

□ **LEE** (Old English, "A meadow"). **LEIGH**.

□ **LEIF** (Old Norse, "Loved one"). Leif Erickson was a Viking explorer who discovered Greenland.

□ **LEIGH** See **LEE**.

□ **LELAND** (Old English, "From the meadowland"). **LEE**.

□ **LENARD** See **LEONARD**.

□ **LEO** (Latin, "The lion"). Thirteen popes have been called Leo. **LEON** Russian: **LEV** (See **LEON, LEONARD, LEOPOLD**).

□ **LEON** French, "Lion-like"). A form of Leo. **LIN, LIONELL** Italian: **LIONELLO**; German: **LEONTIN**.

□ **LEONARD** (Old German, "Lion strong"). Leonardo da Vinci was an inventor, writer, artist, architect and composer. **LEN, LENARD, LENNIE, LENNY** French: **LIENARD**; Italian/Spanish: **LEONARDO, LIONARDO**; German: **LEONHARD**.

□ **LEROY** (Old French, Le Roy, "The king"). **ELROY, LEE, ROY**.

□ **LESLIE** (Scotch, "From the gray stronghold"). A Scottish clan name. **LES, LESLEY**.

□ **LESTER** (Latin, "From the camp"). **LES**.

□ **LEVI** (Hebrew, "Joined in harmony"). The biblical son of Leah and Jacob. **LEVY**.

□ **LINCOLN** (Welsh/Latin, "Lake colony"). **LINK**.

□ **LINDSEY** (Old English, "Linden-tree island"). **LINDSAY**.

☐ **LINUS** *(Greek, "The flaxen haired")*. Linus Pauling, winner of two Nobel Prizes in chemistry and peace.

☐ **LIONEL** *(Old French, "Young lion")*. See **LEON**.

☐ **LIVINGSTON** *(Old Norse, "A loved son")*.

☐ **LLOYD** *(Welsh, "Gray-haired one")*.
FLOYD.

☐ **LOGAN** *(Scotch, "Hollow meadow")*.

☐ **LOMBARD** *(Old German, "Long beard")*.
Italian: **LOMBARDI, LOMBARDO**.

☐ **LON** *(Irish: "Strong")*.
LONNIE, LONNY (See **ALONSO, LAWRENCE**).

☐ **LOREN** See **LAWRENCE**.

☐ **LOUIS** *(Old German, "Warrior prince")*. St. Aloysius is the patron saint of youth/There were18 kings of France named Louis.
ALOIS, LEW, LEWIS, LOU, LOUIE
Latin: **ALOISIUS, LUDOVICUS**; French: **ALOYS, CLOVIS**; Italian: **LODOVICO, LUIGI**; Spanish: **CLODOVEO, LUIS**; Portuguese: **LUIZ**; Dutch: **LODEWICK**; German: **LOTZE, LUDOVIC, LUDWIG**; Swedish: **LUDWIG**.

☐ **LOWELL** *(Old German, "Little wolf")*.
LOVELL, LOWE.

☐ **LUCIUS** *(Latin, "Bringing light")*. Lucius Afranius, a powerful Roman, was put to death by Caesar/ In Semitic religion, Lucifer was the fallen angel who became the "prince of darkness"/There have been many saints Luke, including one of the four evangelists who became the patron saint of doctors and painters.
LUCAS, LUKAS, LUKE French: **LUCE**; Italian: **LUCA, LUCCA, LUCIO**; Spanish: **LUCAS**; German: **LUKAS**; Russian: **LUKA**.

☐ **LUKE** See **LUCIUS**.

☐ **LUTHER** *(Old German, "Illustrious warrior")*. Originally Luther was the name of German emperors/ The name was made popular in modern times by Martin Luther.
LOWTHER, LOTHARIO French: **LOTHAIRE**; Italian: **LOTARIO**; Spanish: **LUTERO**.

☐ **LYLE** *(Old French, "Of the island")*.
LISLE.

☐ **LYNDON** *(Old English, "Linden tree hill")*.
LINDON.

☐ **LYN, LYNN** *(Welsh, "Pool, ' "Waterfall").*

M Most Popular "M" Name. . . **MICHAEL**

☐ **MAC** *(Irish/Scotch, "Son of").* This nickname is usually used for boys whose last names begin with Mac or Mc.
MACK.

☐ **MacKINLEY** *(Irish, "Son of a skillful leader").*

☐ **MADISON** *(Old English, "Son of a powerful soldier").*

☐ **MALACHI** *Hebrew, "Messenger").* The last of the Hebrew prophets, bearer of the Lord's messages/The Irish King Malachi was the friend of Saint Patrick.
MALACHY.

☐ **MALCOLM** *(Scotch, "Disciple of St. Columba", the Scottish saint).*
MAL.

☐ **MALLORY** *(Old French, "The mailed", "Strong").*

☐ **MALVIN** See MELVIN.

☐ **MANFRED** *(Old Germany, "Man of peace").*

☐ **MANNING** *(Old English, "Son of the hero").*

☐ **MANUEL** See EMMANUEL.

☐ **MARC** See MARK.

☐ **MARCUS** See MARK.

☐ **MARCEL** *(Latin, "Little warlike one").*
MARCELLUS Italian: MARCELLO;
Spanish: MARCELO.

☐ **MARIO** *(Latin, "Martial one").*

☐ **MARK** *(Latin, "Of Mars," "A warrior").* In Roman mythology Mars was the god of war and the source of the name Mark/St. Mark is the patron saint of blood and fire and the city of Venice, Italy/One of the four evangelists.
MARCH, MARCIAL, MARCIUS Latin: MARCUS; French: MARC; Italian: MARCO; Spanish: MARCOS; German: MARKUS; Polish: MAREK; Greek: MARKOS.

☐ **MARLEY** *(Old English, "The lake meadow").*

☐ **MARLON** *(Old French, "Little falcon").*
MARLIN (See MERLIN).

☐ **MARLOW** *(Old English, "From the lake by the hill").*
MARLOWE.

☐ **MARSHALL** *(Old French, "Military commander")*.
MARSH, MARSHAL.

☐ **MARTIN** *(Latin, "warlike one")*. In Roman mythology Mars was the god of war/St. Martin divided his cloak with a beggar who later appeared to him as Christ.
MART, MARTEN, MARTIE, MARTY Italian/Spanish: MARTINO.

☐ **MARVIN** *(Old English, "Sea friend")*.
MARV, MARWIN, MYRWYN (See IRVING).

☐ **MASON** *(Latin, "A mason")*.
☒ **MATTHEW** *(Hebrew, "Gift of Jehovah")*. Saint Matthew was one of the twelve apostles and one of the four evangelists.
MATHIAS, MATT, MATTIAS, MATTIE, MATTY French: MATHIEU; Italian: MATTEO; Spanish: MATEO; Danish: MATTHEUS; German: MATTHES, MATTHIA; Polish: MATYAS.

☐ **MAURICE** *(Latin, "The dark")*. A Byzantine emperor/St. Maurice, 3rd Century martyr.
MAURIE, MAURY, MOORE, MORREL, MORIE, MOREY, MORRIE, MORRIS, MORSE Italian: MAURIZIO, MAURO; Spanish: MAURICIO; German: MORITZ; Hungarian: MORICZ; Russian: MORIZ; Scotch: MORRICE.

☐ **MAX** See MAXIMILIAN, MAXWELL.

☐ **MAXIMILIAN** *(Latin, "The greatest")*. Many Roman emperors bore this name as a title, as did the first and last emperor of Mexico.
MAX, MAXIE, MAXIM, MAXY Latin: MAXIMUS; French: MAXIME, MAXIMILIEN; Italian: MASAMO (See MAXWELL).

☐ **MAXWELL** *(Old German, "The greatest")*. Derived from Maximus.
MAC, MAX, MAXIE.

☐ **MAYNARD** *(Old German, "Strength")*.

☐ **MEAD** *(Old English, "The meadow")*.

☐ **MEDWIN** *(Old German, "Powerful friend")*.

☐ **MELVIN** *(Irish, "Sword chief")*.
MEL, MALVIN, MELVYN.

☐ **MENDEL** *(Semitic, "Wisdom")*.
MENDY.

☐ **MERCER** *(English, "A dealer in fabrics")*.

☐ **MEREDITH** *(Old Welsh, "Sea defender")*.

☐ **MERLE** *(French, "A blackbird")*.
MERL.

76

☐ **MERLIN** *(Middle English, "A falcon")*.

☐ **MERRILL** *(Old French, "Famous one")*.

☐ **MERVIN** *(Scotch, "Beautiful sea")*.

☐ **MEYER** *(Germanic, "Overseer"/ Hebrew, "Bringer of light")*.
MYER.

☐ **MICAH** See MICHAEL.

☐ **MICHAEL** *(Hebrew, "Who is like God")*. The Archangel St. Michael was the patron saint of Christian warriors/ The master painter and sculptor Michelangelo Buonarrotti was named for Michael the Angel/The first czar of Russia also bore the name Michael.
MICKEY, MICKIE, MIKE, MITCH, MITCHEL, MITCHELL French: MICHEL; Italian: MICHELE; Spanish: MIGUEL, MIGUELITO; German: MISHA; Swedish: MIKAEL, MIKEL; Russian: MICHAIL, MIKHAIL, MISCHA; Hebrew: MICAH, MIKHAEL, MISHAEL.

☐ **MILES** *(Latin, "Soldier")*.
MYLES Latin: MILO.

☐ **MILO** See MILES.

☐ **MILTON** *(Old English, "From the mill town")*.

☐ **MITCHELL** See MICHAEL.

☐ **MOHAMMED** See MUHAMMAD.

☐ **MONROE** *(Irish, "From the red marsh")*.
MUNRO, MUNROE.

☐ **MONTGOMERY** *(Old French, "From the mountain castle")*.
MONTE, MONTY.

☐ **MORLEY** *(Old English, "The moor meadow")*.

☐ **MORRIS** See MAURICE.

☐ **MORT** See MORTIMER.

☐ **MORTIMER** *(Old French, "From the still water")*.
MORT, MORTIE, MORTY.

☐ **MORTON** *(Old English, "From the moor village")*.
MORT, MORTIE.

☐ **MUHAMMAD** *(Arabic, "Praised")*. The Arab prophet Muhammed founded the Moslem religion/ This name is the most common boys name in the entire world/ There are hundreds of variations including Mahmoud, Mehmet, Ahmad and Mohammad.

☐ **MURDOCK** *(Scotch, "Rich," "from the sea")*.

☐ **MURPHY** *(Irish, "Sea warrior")*.

☐ **MURRAY** *(Scotch, "Mariner")*.

☐ **MYRON** *(Greek, "Fragrant")*. MERYL.

Most Popular "N" Name.... NICHOLAS

☐ **NATHAN** *(Hebrew, "Given of God")*. This name is also a short form of Nathaniel.
NAT, NATE.

☐ **NATHANIEL** *(Hebrew, "Gift of God")*.
NAT, NATE, NATHAN Spanish: NA-TANIEL· Hebrew: NETHANEL.

☐ **NEAL** *(Irish, "Champion")*.
NEIL. NILES, NEALEY Scandinavian: NILS.

☐ **NED** See EDWARD.

☐ **NEIL** See NEAL.

☐ **NELSON** *(English. Neil-son, "Champion's son")*.

☐ **NEMO** *(Greek, "From the glade")*.

☐ **NESTOR** *(Greek, "Aged wisdom")*.

☐ **NEVILLE** *(Old French, "From the new town")*.
NEV, NEVIL.

☐ **NEWELL** *(Latin, "A kernel")*.

☐ **NEWTON** *(Old English, "New town")*.

☐ **NICHOLAS** *(Greek, "Victorious army")*. Possibly the most famous Nicholas, the 4th Century St. Nicholas, Bishop of Myra, became the patron saint of Russia, sailors, young children and merchants/ Santa Claus or Klaus is the German and Dutch for St. Nicholas.
CLAUS, COLAN, COLAS, COLE, CO-LIN, NICK, NICKY, NICHOL French: NICOLE; Spanish/French: NICOLAS; Italian: NICCOLINI, NICOLO; Danish: KALUS, NICOLAUS; Celtic: COLIN; German: KLAUS, NIKLAS, NIKO-LAUS; Russian: NIKOLAI; Greek: NIKOLAOS.

☐ **NIGEL** *(Latin, "Black")*.

☐ **NOEL** *(French, "Born at Christmas")*.
NOWELL Italian: NATALE; Spanish: NATAL.

☐ **NOLAN** *(Irish, "Noble")*.

☐ **NORMAN** *(Middle English, "Man of the North or Norseman")*. Originally, this name meant a Norse or Northman, but with the Norman Conquest in 1066 it came to mean a man from Normandy.
NORM.

□ **NORRIS** *(Old French, "A Norse-man")*. A man from the north, the land of Vikings.

□ **NORTON** *(Old English, "From the north town")*.

□ **NORVIN** *(Old German, "Norse friend")*.
NORWIN.

Most Popular "O" Name...
OWEN

□ **OBADIAH** *(Hebrew, "Servant of the Lord")*.
OBADIAS, OBIE, OBY.

□ **OBERON** *(Old English, "The obedient")*.
AUBERAN.

□ **ODELL** *(Old Norse, "The rich")*.
ODIN.

□ **OGDEN** *(Old English, "From the oak valley")*.

□ **OLAF** *(Old Norse, "Ancestor")*. St. Olaf was the first Christian king of Norway, followed by four other kings of the same name.
OLIN.

□ **OLIVER** *(Latin, "Olive tree"/Old Norse, "Kind")*. In Latin-speaking countries, the olive branch was the symbol of peace/ For the Vikings the name was popularized by King Olaf who became the patron saint of Norway.
NOLL, NOLLY, OLLIE, OLLY French/German: **OLIVIER**; Italian: **OLIVA**; Spanish: **OLIVERIO**.

□ **OMAR** *(Arabic, "Follower of the Prophet")*.

□ **OREN** *(Hebrew, "The pine")*.
ORAN, ORIN.

□ **ORLAN** *(Old English, "From the pointed land")*.
ORLAND.

□ **ORSON** *(Latin, "Like a bear")*.
Italian: URSELLO, URSINO.

□ **ORVILLE** *(Old French, "Gold town")*.

□ **OSCAR** *(Old Norse, "Divine spear")*.
OSSIE, OSSY, OZZY.

□ **OSGOOD** *(Old Norse, "Of godly goodness")*.
OZZIE.

□ **OSMOND** *(Old Norse, "Divine protection")*.

□ **OSWALD** *(Old English, "Divine power").*
OSSIE, OZZIE, WALDO.

□ **OTIS** *(Greek, "Keen hearing").*

□ **OTTO** *(German, "Rich").*
OTHELLO Italian: OTELLO; German: OTHO.

□ **OWEN** *(Welsh, "Young warrior").*
EVAN, EWEN.

Most Popular
"**P**" Name....
PETER

□ **PAGE** *(French, "Youthful attendant").*
PAIGE.

□ **PALMER** *(Latin, "Pilgrim").*

□ **PARKER** *(Middle English, "Park keeper").*
PARK.

□ **PARRY** *(Welsh, "Son of Harry").*
PERRY (See **PERRY**).

□ **PATRICK** *(Latin, "Noble", "Patrician").* The 5th Century English missionary St. Patrick, the patron saint of Ireland, is said to have performed miracles with shamrocks and cleared Ireland of snakes.
PAT, PATSY, PATTIE, PATTY French: PATRICE; Italian: PATRIZIO; Spanish:

PATRICIO; German: PATRIZIUS; Irish: PADDY, PADRAIG.

□ **PATTON** *(Old English, "From the warrior's manor").*
PAT, PATON, PATTEN.

□ **PAUL** *(Latin, "Little").* There have been more than 30 saints Paul, the most famous being Paul, the Apostle. Latin: PAULUS; Italian: PAOLI, PAOLINO, PABOLO; Spanish: PABLO, PAULINO; Portuguese: PAULO; Russian: PAVEL, PAVLENKA; Greek: PAULOS.

□ **PAXTON** *(Old English, "Peace town").*
PAX.

□ **PAYTON** *(Old English, "The fighter's estate").*
PEYTON.

□ **PENROD** *(Old German, "Illustrious chief").*
PEN, ROD, RODDY.

□ **PERRY** *(Anglo-Saxon, "Pear tree"/ Old French, "Little Peter").* See **PETER**.

□ **PETER** *(Latin, "Rock").* The name Jesus gave to Simon the Apostle, who became the keeper of the gates of heaven/ Another St. Peter became the first pope of the Catholic church.

PERKIN, PERRIN, PERRY, PETE, PIERCE, PIERS Latin: **PETRONIUS, PETRUS;** French: **PIERRE, PIERROT;** Italian: **PETRUCCIO, PIERO, PIETRO;** Spanish: **PEDRO;** Swedish: **PER;** Danish: **PEDER;** Dutch: **PIET, PIETER;** German: **PETRUS;** Russian: **PETR, PETRUSCHA;** Greek: **PETROS;** Celtic: **FERRIS.**

☐ **PEYTON** See **PAYTON.**

☐ **PHELPS** *(Old English, "Son of Philip").*

☐ **PHIL** See **PHILIP.**

☐ **PHILIP** *(Greek, "Lover of horses").* St. Philip was one of the twelve Apostles/ Philip the Great colonized the Far East and was the father of Alexander the Great/ Several kings of Spain were named Philip, including Philip II, after whom the Phillipine Islands were named.

PHIL, PHILLY French: **PHILIPPE;** Italian: **FILIPPO;** Spanish: **FELIPE;** German: **PHILIPP;** Swedish: **FILIP;** Greek: **PHILIPPOS.**

☐ **PHINEAS** *(Hebrew, "Oracle").*

☐ **POWELL** *(Welsh, "Son of Howell, lofty").*

☐ **PRENTICE** *(Middle English, "An apprentice").*

☐ **PRESCOTT** *(Old English, "From the priest's cottage").* **SCOTT, SCOTTY.**

☐ **PRESTON** *(Old English, "From the priest's town").*

☐ **PUTNAM** *(Old English, "From the place by the pit").*

☐ **PURVIS** *(Old French, "A purveyor").*

Most Popular "Q" Name...
QUINTON

☐ **QUILLER** *(English, "Writer").*

☐ **QUENTIN** *(Latin, "Fifth child").* **QUINN, QUINT, QUINTIN.**

☐ **QUINCY** *(Old French, "The fifth son's estate")* **QUINN.**

☐ **QUINLAN** *(Irish, "Muscular", "Strong").*

☐ **QUINN** *(Celtic, "The wise").* See **QUENTIN.**

☐ **QUINTON** See **QUENTIN.**

Most Popular "R" Name....
ROBERT

☐ **RADFORD** *(Old English, "The red ford")*.

☐ **RADLEY** *(Old English, "From the red lea")*.

☐ **RAFFERTY** *(Irish, "Prosperous")*.
RAFF.

☐ **RALPH** *(Old English, "Wolf-counsel")*. United Nations official Ralph Bunche won the Nobel Peace Prize in 1950.
RAFE, ROLF, ROLFE, ROLPH French: RAOUL.

☐ **RAMSEY** *(Old English, "Ram's island")*. Ramsey MacDonald, Prime Minister of Great Britain.
RAMSAY.

☐ **RANDALL** See RANDOLPH.

☐ **RANDOLPH** *(Old English, "Shieldwolf")*.
RAND, RANDALL, RANDELL, RANDY.

☐ **RAPHAEL** *(Hebrew, "God heals")*. Raphael was an archangel.
RAFE, RAY Italian: RAFFAELE, RAFFAELLO; Spanish: RAFAEL.

☐ **RAY** *(Latin, "The radiant")*. See RAYMOND.

☐ **RAYMOND** *(Old German, "Mighty protector")*.
RAY French: RAYMOND; Italian: RAIMONDO; Spanish: RAMON; German: RAIMUND.

☐ **RAYNOR** *(Old Norse, "Powerful army")*.
German: RAINER.

☐ **REECE** *(Welsh, "Fiery one")*.
REESE, RHET.

☐ **REED** *(Old English, "Red haired")*.
READ, READE, REID.

☐ **REGAN** *(Latin, "Regal")*.
REAGAN, REAGEN, REGEN.

☐ **REGINALD** *(Old German, "Strong ruler")*.
RAYNOLD, REG, REGGIE, REGGY, REYNOLD, RON, RONALD, RONNIE, RONNY French: REGNAULT, RENAUD, RENE; Italian: RINALDO; Spanish: RENATO, REYNALDOS: German: REINOLD, REINWALD; Scotch: RONALD.

☐ **REUBEN** *(Hebrew, "Behold a son")*. Reuben was the oldest son of Jacob and founder of one of the twelve tribes of Israel.
REUVEN, RUBE, RUBEN, RUBIN.

☐ **REXFORD** *(Old English, "From the king's ford")*.
REX.

☐ **REYNARD** *(Old German, "Mighty")*.
RAY, RAYNARD, RAYNOR, REY, REYNOR French: RENAUD; Italian: RAINARDO; German: REINHARD, REINHARDT.

☐ **RHETT** See REECE.

☐ **RICHARD** *(Old German, "Strong ruler")*. Three kings of England were named Richard, the most famous being Richard the Lionhearted who led the third crusade.
DICK, DICKIE, DICKSON, DICKY, DIXON, RICHARD, RICH, RICHIE, RICK, RICKERT, RICKY, RITCH Italian: RICCARDO, RICCIARDO; Spanish: RICARDO; Scottish: RITCHIE.

☐ **RICHMOND** *(Old German, "King protector")*.
RICHMAN.

☐ **RIPLEY** *(Old English, "From the shouting man's meadow")*.
RIP.

☐ **ROARKE** *(Irish, "Of noted fame")*.
ROURKE.

☐ **ROBERT** *(Old English, "Bright fame")*. Seven saints were named Robert/ King Robert of Scotland made the name famous with help from legendary heroes Rob Roy and Robin Hood.
BOB, BOBBIE, BOBBY, ROB, ROB-BIE, ROBBY, ROBIN, ROBINSON, RUPERT French: ROBINET, RUPERT; Italian: ROBERTO, RUBERTO; Spanish: ROBERTO; German: RUPRECHT; Scotch: RAB, RABBIE, ROBBIE, ROBIN; Irish: RIOBARD.

☐ **ROCHESTER** *(Old English, "From the rocky camp")*.

☐ **ROCKLEY** *(Old English, "From the rocky meadow")*.
ROCK, ROCKY.

☐ **ROCKWELL** *(Old English, "Spring by the rock")*.
ROCK, ROCKY.

☐ **ROD** Short form of names beginning with "Rod".

☐ **RODERICK** *(Old German, "Rich in fame")*.
BRODERICK, ROD, RODDIE, RODDY, RODRICK French: RODRIQUE; Italian/Spanish: RODRIGO; Spanish: RUY; German: RODERICH; Russian: RURICH; Irish: RORY.

☐ **RODNEY** *(Old English, "Famous one's island")*
ROD, RODDY.

☐ **ROGER** *(Old German, "Famous spearman")*. RODGE, RODGER Italian: ROGERO, RUGGIERO; Spanish: ROGERIO; Dutch: RUTGER; German: RUDIGER.

83

☐ **ROLAND** *(Germanic, "Famous land")*.
ORLAND, ROLAND, ROLLAN, ROLLIE, ROLLIN, ROLLO, ROLLY, ROWE, ROWLAND Italian: ORLANDO, ROLANDO; Danish: ROLLAND.

☐ **ROLPH** See RALPH.

☐ **ROMAN** *(Latin, "From Rome")*.

☐ **RONALD** See REGINALD.

☐ **ROOSEVELT** *(German, "From the rose field")*.

☐ **RORY** *(Irish, "Red king")*. See RODERICK.

☐ **ROSCOE** *(Old Norse, "Swift horse")*.
ROSS.

☐ **ROSS** *(Scotch, "From the peninsula")*.

☐ **ROY** *(Old French, "King")*. See LEROY.
French: ROI; Spanish: REYES.

☐ **ROYCE** *(Old English, "Son of the king")*.

☐ **RUBEN** See REUBEN.

☐ **RUDOLPH** *(Old German, "Famous wolf")*. Rudolph I of Hapsburg was the 13th century Holy Roman Emperor.
DOLF, DOLPH, RODOLPH, ROLLO, ROLPH, RUDOLF, RUDIE, RUDY

French: RAOUL, RODOLPHE: Italian/Spanish: RODOLFO; Greek: RODOLPHUS.

☐ **RUDY** See RUDOLPH.

☐ **RUFUS** *(Latin, "The red haired")*.
RUFE Italian: RUFIO.

☐ **RUSS** See RUSSELL.

☐ **RUSTY** See RUSSELL.

☒ **RUSSELL** *(Old French, "Red-haired one")*.
RUSS, RUSTY.

☐ **RUTHERFORD** *(Old English, "From the cattle ford")*.

☒ **RYAN** *(Irish, "Little kIng")*.

☐ **RYLAN** *(Old English, "From the ryeland")*.
RYLAND.

S Most Popular "S" Name.... **STEVEN**

☐ **SALVADOR** *(Latin, "Savior")*.
SAL Italian: SALVATORE; Spanish: XAVIER.

☐ **SAMUEL** *(Hebrew, "His name is God")*. Samuel of the Bible was the first prophet of Israel and a wise judge.
SAM, SAMMY Italian: SAMUELE; Hebrew: SHEMUEL, SHEM.

☐ **SANBORN** *(Old English, "The sandy brook")*.
SANDY.

☐ **SANDOR** See ALEXANDER.

☐ **SANDY** See ALEXANDER.

☐ **SANFORD** *(Old English, "From the sandy ford")*.

☐ **SARGENT** *(Old French, "Officer," "Attendant")*.
SARGE.

☐ **SAUL** *(Hebrew, "The asked for")*.
Saul was the first king of Israel/ Also, Saul of Tarsus later became St. Paul.
SOL, SOLLY, ZOLLY Hebrew: SHAUL.

☐ **SAWYER** *(Middle English, "Wood sawer")*.

☐ **SAXON** *(Old English, "Sword-people")*.
SAX, SAXTON.

☐ **SCOTT** *(Old English, "A Scotchman")*.
SCOTIE, SCOTTY Italian: SCOTTI.

☐ **SEAN** See JOHN.

☐ **SEBASTIAN** *(Latin, "The reverenced")*.
French: BASTIEN, SEBASTIEN; Italian: BASTO, SEBASTIANO; Scandinavian: BASTE; Greek: SEBASTIANOS.

☐ **SELBY** *(Old English, "The manor farm")*.

☐ **SELDON** *(Old English, "The manor valley")*.
SELDEN.

☐ **SERGE** *(Latin, "To serve")*.
Latin: SERGIUS; Spanish: SERGIO; Russian: SERGEI.

☐ **SETH** *(Hebrew, "The appointed")*.
The brother of Cain and Abel; son of Adam and Eve.

☐ **SEYMOUR** *(Old French, "From the town of St. Maur")*.
MORRIE, MORRY.

☐ **SHAMUS** See JAMES.

☐ **SHANE** See JOHN.

☐ **SHAW** *(Old English, "From the grove")*.

☐ **SHAWN** See JOHN.

☐ **SHEA** *(Irish, "Majestic")*.

☐ **SHEAN** *(Irish, "Peaceful little one")*.

☐ **SHELBY** *(Old English, "The ledge estate")*.
SHELLEY.

☐ **SHELDON** *(Old English, "Shield town")*.
SHELL, SHELLEY, SHELTON.

☐ **SHELLEY** See SHELBY, SHELDON.

□ **SHERIDAN** *(Irish, "Wild man")*.

□ **SHERLOCK** *(Old English, "Fairhaired")*.

□ **SHERMAN** *(Old English, "Sheep shearer")*.
MAN, MANNY, SHERM.

□ **SHERWIN** *(Old English, "Quick runner")*.

□ **SHERWOOD** *(Old English, "Bright forest")*.
WOODY.

□ **SIDNEY** *(Phoenician, "From the city of Sidon"/ French, "From St. Denis")*.
SID, SYD, SYDNEY.

□ **SIEGFRIED** *(Old German, "Victory peace")*. The hero of the old German legend, *The Nibelungenlied*.
SIG Italian: SIGEFREDO; German: SIGFRID; Norwegian: SIGVARD.

□ **SIGMUND** *(Old German, "Conquering protection")*. Sigismund was the emperor of Rome in the 15th century.
SIG, SIGMOND, ZIG, ZIGGY French: SIGISMOND; Italian: SIGISMONDO; Spanish: SIGIMUNDO; German: SIGISMUND.

□ **SIMON** *(Hebrew, "The hearing one")*. In the Bible, Simon was one of the twelve disciples of Christ/ There were also nine saints of this name.
SI, SIM, SIMEON Italian: SIMONE; Hebrew: SHIMON.

□ **SINCLAIR** *(French, "From St. Clair, saintly and famous")*.

□ **SKELLY** *(Irish Gaelic, "Historian," "Storyteller")*.

□ **SKIPP** *(Norse, "Ship owner")*.
SKIP, SKIPPER, SKIPPY.

□ **SOLOMON** *(Hebrew, "Peace")*. Biblical: the wisest of the biblical kings/ Shalom, the Hebrew greeting, means "peace".
SOL, SOLLY French: SALOMON; Italian/Spanish: SALOMONE; German: SALOMO; Arabic: SELIM; Hebrew: SHELOMOH.

□ **SORRELL** *(Old French, "Reddish-brown hair")*.

□ **SPARK** *(Middle English, "Gay")*.
SPARKY.

□ **SPENCER** *(Middle English, "Housesteward," "Storekeeper")*.
SPENCE, SPENSER.

□ **STACY** *(Latin, "Firmly established," "Prosperous")*.

□ **STANFORD** *(Old English, "From the rocky ford")*.
STAN.

□ **STANISLAUS** *(Slavic, "Stand of glory", "Glorious position")*. Saint

Stanislaus is patron saint of Poland.
STAN French: **STANISLAS**; Italian: **STANISLAO**; Spanish: **ESTANISLAO**; German: **STANISLAV**.

☐ **STANLEY** *(Old English, "From the rocky meadow")*.
STAN.

☐ **STANTON** *(Old English, "From the rocky farm")*.
STAN.

☐ **STEPHEN** *(Greek, "Crowned one")*. Saint Stephen was the first Christian to die for his faith, the first of eight saints of this name/ The crown of St. Stephen, first king of Hungary, is the symbol of that country.
STEFFEN, STEVE, STEVEN, STEVIE French: **ETIENNE, TIENNOT**; Italian: **STEFANO**; Spanish: **ESTEVAN, ESTEBAN**; Dutch: **STEVIN**; Russian: **STEFAN, STEPKA**; Scottish: **STEENIE**; Greek: **STEPHANOS**.

☐ **STERLING** *(English, "Genuine," "Standard of excellence")*. Early English money was called "sterling."
STIRLING.

☐ **STEVEN** See **STEPHEN**.

☐ **STEWART** *(Old English, "Steward of an estate")*. Stewart was the name of a famous Scottish clan, as well as the family name of a long line of English rulers.
STEW, STU, STUART.

☐ **STUART** See **STEWART**.

☐ **SULLIVAN** *(Irish, "Blackeyed")*.

☐ **SULLY** *(Old English, "The south meadow")*.

☐ **SVEN** *(Norse, "Youthful")*.
SWEN.

☐ **SYDNEY** See **SIDNEY**.

☐ **SYLVESTER** *(Latin, "Of the woods")*.
SILVESTER.

Most Popular "T" Name....
THOMAS

☐ **TAB** *(Old German, "Brilliant")*.
☐ **TAD** See **THADDEUS**.
☐ **TAVIS** *(Scotch Gaelic, "Twin")*. Scotch form of **THOMAS**.
TAVISH.

☐ **TAILOR** *(Middle English, "A tailor")*.

☐ **TERENCE** *(Latin, "Smooth," "Polished")*.
TERRY Spanish: **TERENCIO**.

☐ **TERRY** A familiar form of names beginning in "Ter".

☐ **TEVIS** *(Scotch, "Quick tempered")*.

☐ **THADDEUS** *(Latin, "Praising God")*. Thaddeus was one of the twelve Apostles.
TAD, THAD Italian: **THADDEO**; Spanish: **TADEO**; German: **THADDAUS** (See **JUDAH**).

☐ **THANE** *(Old English, "Attendant")*.

☐ **THEOBALD** *(Old German, "Bold for the people")*.
TYBALT French: **THIBAUD, THIBAUT**; Spanish/Italian: **TEOBALDO**; German: **TIBOLD**.

☐ **THEODORE** *(Greek, "God's gift")*. St. Theodore, the patron saint of Venice, is one of 28 saints named Theodore/ The name gave rise to the royal name Tudor of England.
TAD, TED, TEDDIE, TEDDY, TEODORE, THAD, THEO, TUDOR Italian/Spanish: **TEODORO**; German: **THEODOR**; Russian: **FEDOR**; Greek: **THEODOROS**.

☐ **THOMAS** *(Aramaic, "Twin")*. St. Thomas, one of the Apostles, was said not to have believed that Christ had risen until it was proven to him — hence the expression "a doubting Thomas."
TAMAS, TAMMIE, THOM, THOMA, TOM, TOMA, TOMMIE, TOMMY Italian: **TOMASO**; Spanish: **TOMAS**; German: **THOMA**; Scottish: **TAM, TAMMIE, TAVIS**.

☐ **THORMOND** *(Old English, "Thor's protection")*.
THURMAN, THURMOND.

☐ **THORNE** *(Old English, "Dweller by a thorn tree")*.

☐ **THORNTON** *(Old English, "From the thorny town")*.

☐ **THORSTEIN** See **THURSTON**.

☐ **THURMAN** See **THORMOND**.

☐ **THURSTON** *(Scandinavian, "Thor's stone")*.
THURSTAN Norwegian: **THORSTEIN**.

☐ **TIMON** *(Greek, "Honor," "Reward")*. Shakespeare's play "Timon of Athens" was based on the Greek skeptic philosopher Timon.
TY.

☐ **TIMOTHY** *(Greek, "Honoring God")*. Saint Timothy was a follower of St. Paul.
TIM, TIMMY French: **TIMOTHEE**; Italian: **TIMOTEO**; Russian: **TEEMOFE; TIMOFEI**; Slavic: **TIMOTY**; Greek: **TIMOTHEOS**.

☐ **TOBIAS** *(Hebrew, "God is good")*. **TOBIAH, TOBY** French: **TOBIE**; Italian: **TOBIA**.

☐ **TOBY** See TOBIAS.

☐ **TODD** *(Scottish, "Fox")*.

☐ **TONY** See ANTHONY.

☐ **TOREY** *(Anglo-Saxon, "High")*.

☐ **TORIN** *(Irish, "Chief")*.

☐ **TRACY** *(Latin, "Bold, courageous one")*.
TRACIE.

☐ **TRAVIS** *(Old French, "From the crossroads")*.
TRAVERS.

☐ **TRENT** *(Latin, "Rapid stream")*.

☐ **TREVOR** *(Irish, "Prudent")*.
Welsh: TREFOR.

☐ **TRISTAN** *(Old Welsh, "Noisy")*.
A knight of the Round Table.
TRIS.

☐ **TROY** *(Old French, "Curly haired")*.

☐ **TRUMAN** *(Old English, "Faithful one")*.

☐ **TUCKER** *(Middle English, "A tucker of cloth")*.

☐ **TURNER** *(Middle English, "Lathe worker")*.

☐ **TYLER** *(Middle English, "A tile maker")*.
TY.

☐ **TYRONE** *(Greek, "Sovereign")*.
Tyr was the chief god in Norse mythology.
TY.

☐ **TYRUS** *(Greek, "From the city of Tyre")*.
TY.

☐ **TYSON** *(Old French, "Son of the Teuron")*.
TY.

Most Popular
"U" Name....
URIAH

☐ **ULRIC** See ALARIC.

☐ **UDELL** *(Old Eagle, "From the yew-tree valley")*.

☐ **ULYSSES** *(Greek, "Vengeful")*.
Latin form of the Greek Odysseus/ The wise adventurer in Homer's *Odyssey*.

☐ **UPTON** *(Old English, "From the hill town")*.

☐ **URBAN** *(Latin, "From the city")*.
Eight popes were named Urban.
ORBAN French: URBAIN; Russian: URVAN.

☐ **URIAH** *(Hebrew, "My light is Jehovah," "Flame of Jehovah")*. Captain in King David's army and husband of Bathsheba.

☐ **URIEL** *(Hebrew, "Flame of God")*. One of the Archangels.

☐ **UZZIAH** *(Hebrew, "The Lord's might")*.

Most Popular
"V" Name....
VINCENT

☐ **VAIL** *(Middle English, "From the valley")*.

☐ **VAL** *(Latin, "Strong")*. Short form for names beginning with Val.

☐ **VALDEMAR** *(Old German, "Famous ruler")*.

☐ **VALENTINE** *(Latin, "Strong," "Healthy," "Valorous")*. St. Valentine became a martyr on Feb. 14th.
VAL, VALENTE, VALIANT French/Spanish/German: VALENTIN; Italian: VALENTINO.

☐ **VAN** *(Dutch, "From," or "Of")*. A nickname given those with Dutch surnames beginning with "Van."

☐ **VANCE** *(Middle English, "Thresher")*. A van or fan is an instrument used for threshing.

☑ **VAUGHN** *(Old Welsh, "Small one")*.
VAUGHAN, VON.

☐ **VERN** See **VERNON**.

☐ **VERNON** *(Latin, "Springlike")*.
VERN, VERNE.

☐ **VICK** See **VICTOR**.

☐ **VICTOR** *(Latin, "Conqueror")*. The name of three popes and 35 saints.
VIC, VICK French: VICTOIR; Italian: VITTORIO.

☐ **VINCENT** *(Latin, "Conquering one")*.
VIN, VINCE, VINNY French/German: VINCENZ; Italian: VINCENZO; Hungarian: VINCZE; Polish: VINCENTY.

☐ **VIRGIL** *(Latin, "The staff of authority")*.
VIRGE Italian/Spanish: VIRGILIO.

☐ **VLADIMIR** *(Slavic, "Prince of the world")*.
VLAD.

Most Popular
"W" Name...
WILLIAM

☐ **WADE** *(Old English, "One who moves forward")*. In Norse mythology, Wade was the spirit of storms.

☐ **WAGNER** *(German, "Wagon maker").*

☐ **WAINWRIGHT** *(Old English, "Wagon maker").*

☐ **WALDEMAR** *(Old German, "Famous ruler").* A 12th Century king. WALDO, WALLY Scandinavian: VALDEMAR.

☐ **WALDEN** *(Old English, "From the forest"/Old German, "Ruler").*

☐ **WALDO** *(Old German, "One who rules").* German: VALDO (See **WALDEMAR**).

☐ **WALKER** *(Old English, "A fuller of cloth").* An occupational name. WALLY.

☐ **WALLACE** *(Old English, "A foreigner," "A man from Wales").* WAL, WALLIS, WALLY, WALSH, WELCH, WELSH German: WALACHE, WALLACHE: Slavic: VLACH.

☐ **WALLY** A short form for names beginning with "Wal".

☐ **WALT** A short form of names beginning with "Walt."

☐ **WALTER** *(Old German, "Powerful warrior," or "Ruling the people").* WALLY, WALT, WATT French: GAUTHIER, GAUTIER; Italian: GUALTIERO; Spanish: GUITTIERE; German: WALTHER.

☐ **WALTON** *(Old English, "The walled town").*

☐ **WARD** *(Old English, "Watchman").* WARDEN.

☐ **WARREN** *(Old German, "Watchman", "Protector").* A warden.

☐ **WASHINGTON** *(Old English, "From the town of the wise").*

☐ **WAYLAND** *(Old German, "From the land by the highway").* WAYLEN, WAYLON German: WIELAND.

☐ **WAYNE** See WAINWRIGHT.

☐ **WEBSTER** *(Old English, "A weaver").* WEAVER, WEBB German: WEBER.

☐ **WELLINGTON** *(Old English, "From the prosperous estate").*

☐ **WENDELL** *(Old German, "Wanderer").* German: WENDE.

☐ **WERNER** *(Old German, "Defending warrior").* A German form of WARNER.

☐ **WESLEY** *(Old English, "From the west meadow").* WES, WESTLEY.

☐ **WESTCOTT** *(Old English, "From the west cottage").*

☐ **WESTON** *(Old English, "From the west town").*
WES.

☐ **WEYLIN** *(Irish, "Wolf's son").*

☐ **WHITLEY** *(Old English, "From the white lea or meadow").*

☐ **WHITMORE** *(Old English, "From the white moor").*

☐ **WHITNEY** *(Old English, "From the white island").*

☐ **WILBERT, WILBUR** See GILBERT.

☐ **WILFORD** *(Old English, "From the willow ford").*
GUILFORD.

☐ **WILFRED** *(Old German, "Resolute peacemaker").*

☐ **WILHELM** German form of WILLIAM.

☐ **WILL** *(Old English, "Resolute").* Also a short form for all names beginning with "Wil."
WILLIE, WILLY.

☐ **WILLARD** *(Old German, "Determined").*
WILL, WILLIE.

☐ **WILLIAM** *(Old German, "Resolute protector").* William the Conqueror, King of England after the Norman Conquest in 1066, gave the name its great popularity.
BILL, BILLIE, BILLY, WILKES, WILL, WILLET, WILLIE, WILLIS, WILLY, WILSON French: GUILLAUME; Italian: GUGIELMO; Spanish: GUILLERMO; Dutch: WILLEM; German: WILHELM; Swedish: VILHELM.

☐ **WILTON** *(Old English, "From the well farm").*
WILLIE, WILT.

☐ **WINFIELD** *(Old English, "Friendly field").* Gen. Winfield Scott, U.S. Army.

☐ **WINSLOW** *(Old English, "From the friend's hill").* Winslow Homer, American painter.

☐ **WINSTON** *(Old English, "From the friend's town").* Winston Churchill.
WIN, WINNIE, WINNY, WINTON.

☐ **WINTHROP** *(Old English, "From the friendly village").* Winthrop Rockefeller.

☐ **WOODROW** *(Old English, "From the hedgerow").* Woodrow Wilson, 28th President.
WOODY.

☐ **WOODWARD** *(Old English, "Forest ranger").*

☐ **WOODY** A familiar form of names containing "Wood".

Name Me, I'm Your Daughter!

Most Popular "A" Name.... **AMANDA**

☐ **ABIGAIL** *(Hebrew, "My father is joy")*. Abigail Adams was the wife of President John Adams/ A wife of King David known as the "handservant of the Lord".
ABBEY, ABBIE, GAIL, GALE, GAY, GAYLE (See **GAIL, GALE**) Irish: **ABAIGEAL**.

☐ **ACANTHA** *(Greek, "Thorned")*. Legendary mother of Apollo.

☐ **ADA** *(German, "Happy," or "Prosperous")*. St. Ada, 7th Century French abbess
ADAH, ADDIE, ADI, AIDA.

☐ **ADELA, ADELLA** *(Old German Adal, "Noble one")*. Adela Rogers St. John, U.S.writer. See **ADELAIDE**.

☐ **ADELAIDE** *(Old German, "Of noble rank")*. A name of German royalty since the 10th century.
ADDA, ADDIE, ADDY, ADEL, ADELINE, ADELAIDA, ADELAIS, ADELIA, ADELICIA, ADELINA, ADELISA, ADELIZA, ALEEN, ALINE, ALISA, DEL, DELLA, DELLY, EDELINE, HEIDI French: **ADELE, ADELINE, ADELL**; Italian/Spanish: **ADELAIDA**; German: **ADELHEID, ADELINE, ODILE**.

☐ **ADINA** *(Hebrew, Adin, "Voluptuous")*.
ADENA, ADINE, DINA.

☐ **ADONIA** *(Greek, Fem. of Adonis, "Beautiful woman")*. The festival of Adonia was celebrated by all Greek women.

☐ **ADORA** *(Greek, "A gift")*.
ADOREE, DORA, DORI.

☐ **ADRIENNE** *(Latin, "From the city of Adria")*.
ADREA, ADRENA, ADRIA, ADRIANA, ADRIEL, ADRIELLA, HADRIA.

☐ **AGATHA** *(Greek, "Kind and good")*. St. Agatha, patroness of Sicily, who legend says saved her city from the eruption of Mt. Etna.
AGATE, AGATHE, AGGIE, AGGY Italian/Spanish/Swedish: AGATA; Russian: AGAFIA.

☐ **AGNES** *(Greek, "Pure")*. Six saints were named Agnes.
AGGIE, AGNA, AGNESSE, AGNETA, ANNIS, NESSIE, NESSY Irish: INA; French: AGNIES; Italian: AGNELLA, AGNESCA, AGNESE, AGNOLA; Spanish: INES, INESILA, INEZ; Russian: AGNESSA, NESSA; Swedish: AGNETA; Slavic: NEYSA, NEZIKA.

☐ **AILEEN** See HELEN.

☐ **AIRLIA** *(Greek, "Ethereal")*.

☐ **ALANNA** *(Irish, Fem. of Alan, "Comely and fair")*.
ALANA, ALANAH, ALAINE, ALANE, ALLEEN, ALLINA, ALLYN, LANA.

☐ **ALARICE** *(Old German, Fem. of Alaric, "Ruler of all")*.
ALARICA, ALRICA, ELRICA.

☐ **ALBERTA** *(Old English, Fem. of Albert, "Noble, bright")*.
ALBERTINA, ALBERTINE, ALI, ALVERTA, BERTA, BERTE, BERTIE, ELBERTA, ELBERTINE French: AUBERTA.

☐ **ALCINA** *(Greek, "Strong-minded")*.
ALCINE.

☐ **ALDIS** *(Old English, "From the old house")*.
ALDYS.

☐ **ALDORA** *(Old English, "Of noble rank")*.

☐ **ALETHEA** *(Greek, "Truthful")*.
See ALICE.

☐ **ALEXA** See ALEXANDRA.

☐ **ALEXANDRA** *(Greek, "Helper of mankind")*.
ALESSA, ALEXA, ALEXANDRIA, ALEXANDRINA, ALEXANDRINE, ALEXINA, ALEXINE, ALEXIS, LEXINE, LEXIE, SANDRA, SANDY, SONDRA, ZANDRA, ZANDY French: ALEXANDRINE; Italian: ALESSANDRA; Spanish: ALEJANDRA; Russian: SACHA, SASHA.

☐ **ALEXIS** See ALEXANDRIA.

☐ **ALFREDA** *(Old English, "Elf, counselor")*.
ALFIE, ALFRETA, ELFREDA, ELFRIDA, ELFRIEDA, ELVA, FREDA.

☐ **ALI** Short for names beginning with "Al".

☐ **ALICE** *(Greek, "Truth")*.
ALECIA, ALEECE, ALETA, ALETHEA,

96

ALICIA, ALICIENNE, ALIS, ALISA, ALISON, ALLIS, ALISSA, ALIX, ALLIE, ALYCE, ALLYCE, ALLYSA, ELSIE, LISSA, LISSY French/German: ADELICIA, ALIX; Italian/Spanish: ALICIA; Danish: ELSE; Swedish: ELSA.

☐ **ALINA** *(Celtic, "Fair")*.

☑ **ALISON** *(Irish, Allsun, "Little truthful one")*.
ALLISON. See ALICE.

☐ **ALISA** *(Hebrew, "Joy")*.

☐ **ALMA** *(Spanish, "The soul")*.
ALIMNA.

☐ **ALMIDA** *(Welsh, "Shapely")*.

☐ **ALMIRA** See ELMIRA.

☐ **ALPHA** *(Greek, "The first")*.
ALFA.

☐ **ALTHEA** *(Greek, "Healer")*.
ALTHEDA, ELTHEA, ELTHA, THEA.

☐ **ALURA** *(Old English, "Elf peace")*.

☑ **ALYSSA** *(Greek, the fragrant alyssum flower, "Rational")*. See ALICE.

☐ **AMABEL** *(Latin, "Lovable")*.
AMA, AMABELLE, BELLE, MAB.

☐ **AMADEA** *(Latin, "Love of God")*.
AMADEE.

☐ **AMANDA** *(Latin, "Lovably esteemed")*.
MANDA, MANDALINE, MANDY French: AMANDINE.

☐ **AMBER** *(Old French, "The amber jewel")*.

☐ **AMELIA** *(Teutonic, "A zealous worker")*.
AMALEA, AMALIA, AMELINE, AMELITA, AMY. (See AMY, EMILY, EMMA.) French: AMELIE.

☐ **AMELINDA** *(Latin, "Beloved and beautiful")*.

☐ **AMY** *(Latin, "Beloved")*.
AME, AMELITA, AMIE, AMI, AMICIA, AMICE. (See AMELIA, EMILY.) French: AIMCE, AMORETTE; Italian: AMORETTA; Spanish: AMORITA.

☐ **ANASTASIA** *(Greek, "Of the Resurrection")*.
ANSTICE, STACEY, STACIA, STACIE, STACY. French: ANASTASIE; Irish: STACY.

☐ **ANDA** *(Old Norse, "A breath")*.

☐ **ANDREA** *(Greek, Fem. of Andreas and Andrew, "Womanly")*.
ANDRIA, ANDREANA, ANDRIANA. French: ANDREE; Greek: ANDRINA.

☐ **ANGELA** *(Greek, "Messenger", "Angelic")*.
ANGEL, ANGELICA, ANGELINA, AN-

GELINE, ANGELITA, ANGIE, ANGY. French: ANGELIQUE; Italian: ANGIOLA, ANGIOLETTA.

☐ **ANITA** See ANN, ANNE.

☐ **ANN, ANNE** *(Hebrew, Hannah, "Grace")*. From Hannah, the Biblical mother of Samuel/ St. Anna was the mother of the Virgin Mary.
ANA, ANETTE, ANIA, ANITA, ANITRA, ANNA, ANNABEL, ANNABELLA, ANNABELLE, ANNETTA, ANNETTE, ANNICE, ANNIE, ANNY, ANUSKA, ANYA, HANNA, HANNAH, HANNI, HANNY, NAN, NANA, NANCE, NANCY, NANETTE, NANNIE, NANNY, NETTIE, NINA, NINETTE, NITA, (See also POLLYANNA) French: NANON, NINON; Italian: ANNICA, NANNA; Spanish: ANITA; Danish: ANNIKA; Dutch: ANTJE; German: ANNCHEN, HANNE; Hungarian: NANI; Russian: ANNINKA, ANNUSCHKA; Scotch: ANNOR, NANTY.

☐ **ANSELMA** *(Old Norse, Fem. of Anselm, "protected by God")*.
SELMA, ZELMA.

☐ **ANTOINETTE** *(Latin, Fem. of Anthony, "Priceless")*.
ANTONIA, ANTONINA, NETTIE, NETTY, TONI, TONIA, TONY French: ANTONIE; Italian: ANTONIETTA.

☐ **APRIL** *(Latin, "To open up")*.
APRILETTE, AVERIL, AVRIL.

☐ **ARDELLE** *(Latin, "Zealous," "Ardent")*.
ARDA, ARDEEN, ARDELIA, ARDELIS, ARDELLA, ARDENE, ARDINE, ARDIS.

☐ **ARDIS** See ARDELLE.

☐ **ARETA** *(Greek, "Excellence," "Virtue")*. From the Grecian Fountain Arethusa.
ARETTA, ARETTE, ARETHA.

☐ **ARETHA** See ARETA.

☐ **ARIANA** *(Greek, Ariadna, "Of Aries")*. The mythological princess of ancient Crete.

☐ **ARIEL** *(Hebrew, "Lioness of God")*.
ARIELLA, ARIELLE.

☐ **ARLENE** *(Irish, "A pledge")*.
ARLANA, ARLEEN, ARLENA, ARLETA, ARLETTE, ARLINA, ARLINE, LENA, LINA German: ERLINE.

☐ **ARMINA** *(Old German, "Warrior maid," Fem. of Herman, "Warrior")*.
ARMANDINE, ARMANTINE, ARMEDA, ARMINA, ARMINE, ARMINDA, ARMINDE, ARMINTA, ARMANTINE, ERMA, ERMINA, ERMELINDA, HERMA, HERMINE, HERMILIA, IRMA, IRMADEL (See HERMIONE) French: ARMANDE.

☐ **ASHLEY** (*Old English*, *"Ash tree meadow"*).

☐ **ASTA** (*Greek*, *"The star"*). Astraea was both the Greek and Roman goddess of justice.
ASTRA, ASTREA, ASTRED, ASTRELLA Scand.:AASTA; Greek: ASTRAEA

☐ **AUDREY** (*Old English*, *"Noble strength"*).
ADDY, AUDRA, AUDREA, AUDRIE, AUDRY.

☐ **AURELIA** (*Latin*, *"Golden"*). In Roman mythology the goddess of the dawn.
AUREA, AUREL, AURILLA, ORALEE, ORALIA, OREL, ORELEE, ORIANA, ORIEL, ORLENA, ORLENE, ORIETTE French/German: AURELIE; Italian/Spanish: AURELIA.

☐ **AURORA** (*Latin*, *"The dawn"*).
ORA, RORA, RORY French/German: AURORE; Slavic: ZORA.

B Most Popular "B" Name....
BARBARA

☐ **BAMBI** (*Italian*, *"Little baby"*).
BAMBALINA, BIMMI.

☐ **BARBARA** (*Greek*. *"Stranger"*, *"Foreigner"*). The name of four virgin saints/Patroness of thunder and modern gunfire.
BAB, BABA, BABETTE, BABITA, BABS, BAR, BARB, BARBEE, BARBETTE, BARBEY, BARBI, BARBICA, BARBIE, BARBRA, BARBY, BOBBIE, BOBBY, BONNIE, BONNY Russian: VARA, VARINA, VARINKA.

☐ **BARBIE** See BARBARA.

☐ **BEA** See BEATRICE.

☐ **BEATRICE** (*Latin*, *"She who brings joy"*).
BEA, BEATRISSA, BEATTIE, TRIX, TRIXIE, TRIXY Italian: BICE; Spanish/German: BEATRIX; Russian: BEATRIKS; Slavic: BEATRICIA; Scotch: BEITRIS.

☐ **BECKY** See REBECCA.

☐ **BELINDA** (*Old Spanish*, *"Beautiful"*).
BELLE, LINDA.

☐ **BELLA** See BELLE.

☐ **BELLANCA** (*Italian*, *"Blonde"*).
BIANCA Spanish: BLANCA.

☐ **BELLE** (*French*, *"Beautiful"*).
BELL, BELLA, BELVA.

☐ **BERDINE** (*Old German*, *"Glorious"*).

☐ **BERENICE** *(Greek, "Bringer of victory")*. The royal name of ancient Egypt and Syria/ The daughter of Herod.
BERNICE, BERNIE, BERNY, BUNNY, NIKKI, NIXIE, (See **VERONICA**) French: **VERONIQUE**; German: **VERONIKE**.

☐ **BERNADETTE** *(French, Fem. of Bernard, "Brave bear")*.
BERNA, BERNADINE, BERNADOTTE, BERNARDINE, BERNETTA, BERNETTE, BERNIE, BERNITA Italian/Spanish: **BERNARDINA**.

☐ **BERTHA** *(Old German, "The bright one")*.
BERTA, BERTE, BERTIE, BERTINA, BERTINE, BIRDIE, BIRDY.

☐ **BESS** See **ELIZABETH**.

☑ **BETH** See **ELIZABETH**.

☐ **BETHANY** *(Hebrew, "House of poverty")*. Also a village near Jerusalem.

☐ **BETSY** See **ELIZABETH**.

☐ **BETTE, BETTY** See **ELIZABETH**.

☐ **BEVERLY** *(Old English, "From the beaver's meadow")*.
BEV, BEVIE, BUFFY.

☐ **BIANCA** See **BELLANCA**, BLANCHE.

☐ **BILLIE** See **WILHELMINA**.

☐ **BLANCA** See **BELLANCA**, BLANCHE.

☐ **BLANCHE** *(Old French, "White, fair one")*.
BELLANCA Italian: **BIANCA**; Spanish: **BLANCA**; German: **BLANKA**; Irish: BLINNIE.

☐ **BLAIR** See the male name BLAIR.

☐ **BLYTHE** *(Old English, "Cheerful")*.

☑ **BONNIE** *(Latin, "Good")*.
BONA, BONNA, BONITA, BUNNY.

☐ **BRANDY** An American pet name.

☐ **BRENDA** *(Irish, "A firebrand," "Sword")*.

☐ **BRENNA** *(Irish, "Raven")*.

☐ **BRIANA** *(Irish, Fem. of Brian, "Strong")*.
BRINA, BRIANNE, BRYANA.

☐ **BRIDGET** *(Irish, "The mighty")*. Goddess of wisdom in Irish myth/ The female patron saint of Ireland.
BIRGIT, BIRGITTA, BRIGANTIA, BRIGETTE, BRIGITTA, BRITA French: BRIGITTE; Swedish: **BIRGETTA**; Irish: BIDDY, BRIETTA, BRIGITA; Scotch: BRIDE.

☐ **BROOKE** *(English, "The brook")*.

☐ **BUNNY** See **BERENICE, BONNIE.**

Most Popular
"C" Name....
CHRISTINA

☐ **CALANDRA** *(Greek, "The lark")*.
CAL, CALLIE, CALLY French: CALANDRE; Spanish: CALANDRIA.

☐ **CALANTHA** *(Greek, "Beautiful flower")*.
CAL, CALANTHE, CALLIE, CALLY.

☐ **CALISTA** *(Greek, "The most beautiful")*. The Callisto of Greek myth was the beauty beloved of Zeus.
CALESTA, CALIXTA, CALLIE, CALLISTA, CALLISTE Greek: CALLISTO.

☐ **CAMILLA** *(Latin, "Attendant at religious ceremonies")*. In Roman mythology, Camilla was Diana's attendant/ In Virgil's *Aeneid*, Camilla was a queen.
CAM, CAMELLA, CAMMY, MILLY French: CAMILLE; Spanish: CAMILA.

☐ **CAMILLE** See **CAMILLA.**

☐ **CANDACE** *(Greek, "Dazzling white," "Pure")*. A title of the queens of ancient Egypt.

☐ **CANDIDA** *(Latin, "Dazzling white")*.
CANDIDE, CANDY.

☐ **CANDRA** *(Latin, "Shining")*.

☐ **CARA** *(Latin, "Dear one")*.
CARILLA, CARINE, CARRIE Spanish: CARITA.

☐ **CARINA** *(Latin, "The keel")*.
CARIN, CARINE, CARINNA.

☐ **CARISSA** *(Latin, "Loving")*.
CHARISSA.

☐ **CARLA** See **CHARLOTTE.**

☐ **CARLIE, CARLY** See **CAROLINE, CHARLOTTE.**

☐ **CARMA** *(Hindu, Karma, "Destiny")*.

☐ **CARMEN** *(Latin, "A song")*.
CARMINA, CARMINE, **CARMITA,** CHARMAIN, CHARMAINE Spanish: CARMENCITA.

☐ **CAROL** *(Latin, Fem. of Charles and Carl, "Strong and womanly"/ Also Old French, "To sing with joy")*. Charlotte was the name of queens of England and Savoy.
CAREY, CARI, CARLA, CARLEN, CARLENE, CARLIN, CARLINA, CARLINE, CARLITA, CARLOTA, CARLOTTA, CARLY, CARO, CAROLA, CAROLE, CAROLIN, CAROLINE, CAROLYN, CARRIE, CARROLL, CARY, CARYL,

CHARLA, CHARLEEN, CHARLENE, CHARLINA, CHARLOTTA, CHARMAIN, CHARMAINE, CHARMIAN, CHARMION, CHERYL, CHERLYN, KAREL, KARI, KARLA, KARLEN, KARLENE, KARLOTTA, KAROLE, KAROLY, LOLA, LOLITA, LOTTA, LOTTI, LOTTIE, SHARLET, SHARYL, SHEREE, SHARLEEN, SHARLENE, SHERRIE, SHERRY, SHERYL French: **CHARLOTTE**; Italian: **CAROLINA**; Spanish: **CAROLINA**; German: **KAROLINE, LINA, LOTTCHEN**. (See **CHARLOTTE**).

☐ **CAROLINE** See CAROL.

☐ **CARRIE** See CAROL.

☐ **CASEY** (*Irish, "Brave"*).

☐ **CASSANDRA** (*Greek, "Helper of men"*). In Greek mythology she was a princess endowed with the gift of prophecy though no one believed her. CASS, CASSIE, CASSY, SANDY French: **CASSANDRE**; Greek: **KASSANDRA**.

☐ **CASSIE** See CASSANDRA.

☐ **CATHERINE** (*Greek, "Pure"*). Six great saints, queens of England and Spain, and the Empress of Russia, have made this one of the most popular female names in history. CAITLYN, CASS, CASSY, CAT, CATARINA, CATE, CATHA, CATHARINA, CATHARINE, CATHIE, CATHY, KATE, KATHERINE, KATHY, KATRIN, KAY, KAYE, KETTI, KIT, KITTY, RINA, TINKA, TRINA Italian: **CATERINA**; Spanish: **CATALINA**; Swedish: **KATARINA**; Norwegian: **KARENA, KARIN**; Swiss: **KATHRI, TRINE**; Hungarian: **KATI**; Polish: **KASSIA, KASIA**; Russian: **EKATERINA, KATINKA, KATUSCHA, KATUSHKA, KATYA**; Slavic: **KATKA**, Irish: **CAITLIN, CATHLEEN, KATHLEEN, KATTY**; Scotch: **KATIE**; Danish: **KATHRINA, KATRINE, KATRINKA, KARIN, KARINA, KAREN**.

☐ **CATHLEEN** See CATHERINE.

☐ **CECILIA** (*Latin, Fem. of Cecil, "Dim sighted"*). St. Cecilia is the female patron saint of music. CELIA, CECILY, CICELY, CICILY, CIS, CISSIE, SIS, SISELY, SISSIE, SISSY French: **CECILE**; German: **CACILIA, CECILIE**; Irish: **SHEELAH, SHEILA, SHEILAH, SHELAGH**.

☐ **CECILY** See CECILIA.

☐ **CELENA** See CELESTE.

☐ **CELENE** See CELESTE.

☐ **CELESTE** (*Latin, "Heavenly"*). CELENE, CELENA, CELESTA, CELESTINA, CELESTINE, CELIA.

☐ **CELINA** See SELENA.

☐ **CHARITY** *(Latin, Caritas, "Benevolent")*.
CHARISSA, CHARITA, CHERRY Italian/Irish: CARA.

☐ **CHARLEEN** See CAROL, CHARLOTTE.

☐ **CHARLOTTE** *(French, "Little womanly one")*. See CAROL.

☐ **CHARMAIN** See CARMEN.

☐ **CHASTITY** *(Latin, "A Puritan virtue name")*.

☐ **CHER** *(French, "Beloved")*.
CHERI, CHERIE, SHER, SHERRY.

☐ **CHERIE** *(French, "Cherished and beloved")*. See CHER.

☐ **CHERRY** *(Old French, "Like a cherry")*. See CHARITY.

☐ **CHLOE** *(Greek, "Young grass")*. A name for Demeter, the goddess of the new wheat.

☐ **CHLORIS** *(Greek, "Pale flower")*.
CLORIS.

✓☑ **CHRISTINE** *(Greek, "Christian")*. Originally a Greek name to honor Christ.
CHRISSIE, CHRISSY, CHRISTA, CHRISTIANA, CHRISTIANE, CHRISTINA, CRIS, CRISSIE, CRISSY, CRISTINE, KRISTIN Italian/Spanish: CRISTINA; Danish: KARSTIN; German: KRISTAL, STINA, STINE; Scandinavian: KIRSTE, KIRSTEN, KIRSTIN,KRISTA; Scotch: CAIRISTIONA, CHRISTEL, CHRISTIE, KIRSTIE; Slavic: KRISTINA.

☐ **CHRISTIE** See CHRISTINE.

☐ **CICELY** See CECILIA.

☐ **CINDY** See CYNTHIA, LUCINDA.

☐ **CISSIE** See CECILIA.

☐ **CLAIRE** See CLARA.

☐ **CLARA** *(Latin, "Bright," "Illustrious")*. St. Clare of Assisi was a friend and assistant of St. Francis/ Clara Barton founded the American Red Cross.
CLAIR, CLAIRINE, CLARE, CLARENDA, CLARETTA, CLAROTTE, CLARI, CLARICE, CLAREY, CLARIN, CLARINA, CLARINDA, CLARITA, CLARISSA, CLARY French: CLAIRE, CLAIRETTE, CLARICE; Italian: CHIARA; German: KLARA.

☐ **CLARICE** See CLARA.

☐ **CLARISSA** See CLARA.

☐ **CLAUDIA** *(Latin, Fem. of Claudius and Claude, "The lame")*.
CLAUDIE, CLAUDINE French: CLAUDE, CLAUDETTE; Spanish: CLAUDINA.

☐ **CLEA** See CLEO.

□ **CLEMENCY** *(Latin, Fem. of Clement, "The merciful")*. Clementia was a Roman goddess.
CLEMENCE, CLEMENTIA, CLEMMY French: **CLEMENTINE**; Italian: **CLEMENZA**; Danish: **CLEMENTINA**; German: **KLEMENTINE**.

□ **CLEMENTINE** See CLEMENCY.

□ **CLEO** *(Greek, "Famed")*. Originally used to honor Cleopatra.

□ **CLYDIA** *(Greek, Fem. of Clyde, "Glorious")*.
CLYDINA, CLYDINE, GLYDIA.

□ **COLETTE** See Nicole.

□ **COLLEEN** *(Irish, "Girl")*.
COLLINE, COLLYO.

□ **CONNIE** See CONSTANCE.

☑ **CONSTANCE** *(Latin, Fem. of Constantine, "Constant")*. Originally used to honor the Emperor Constantine/ The Puritans also used it as a virtue name.
CONNIE, CONNY, CONSTANCY, CONSTANTIA, CONSTANTINA, CONSTANTINE Italian/Spanish: **CONSTANZA**; German: **KONSTANZE**; Russian: **KOSTANCIA, STANCA.**

□ **CORA** *(Greek, "Maiden")*. Kore (or Persephone) in Greek myth was the daughter of the goddess Demeter.
CARELLA, CORENA, CORENE, CORETTA, CORETTE, COREY, CORIE, CORRENA, CORRIE, CORRY, KORA French: **CORINNE**; Spanish: **CORINA**; Greek: **KORE.**

□ **CORAH** *(Hindu, "the unchanging")*.

□ **CORAL** *(Latin, "The rock")*. Coral from the Mediterranean Sea was worn in ancient times as a protective amulet.
CORALINA, CORALINE French: **CORALIE.**

□ **CORRINE** See CORA.

□ **CORISSA** *(Greek, "Maidenly")*.
CORISA.

□ **CORNELIA** *(Latin, Fem. of Cornelius, "The cornel tree")*. The cornel tree that was devoted to Apollo in Greek mythology/ In ancient Rome Cornelia was the famous mother of noted sons.
CORNELA, CORNELLA, CORNELE, CORNIE, NEILA, NELLA, NELIE, NELL, NILA French: **CORNELIE.**

□ **COSIMA** *(Greek, Fem. of Cosmo, Kosmos, "Order")*.

□ **COURTNEY** *(English, "Of the court")*.

□ **CRYSTAL** *(Latin, "A clear jewel")*.
CHRYSTAL.

□ **CYBIL** See SIBYL.

□ **CYNTHIA** *(Greek, "The moon")*. A title of Artemis, Greek goddess of the moon, honoring her birthplace, Mount Cynthus.
CINDA, CINDY, CYNTHIE, CYNTHY Greek: KYNTHIA.

D Most Popular "D" Name . . . **DAWN**

□ **DACIA** *(Latin, "From Dacia")*. An ancient Roman "place" name for the region north of Danube.
DACEY.

□ **DAGMAR** *(Danish, "Glory of the Danes")*. Dagmar was a Queen of Denmark.

□ **DAHLIA** *(Old Norse, "From the valley")*. The dahlia flower was named for a Swedish botanist named Dahl.
DALIA.

□ **DAISY** *(Old English, "The day's eye")*.
DAISIE.

□ **DALE** *(Old English, Dael, "The valley")*.
DAYLE.

□ **DALLAS** *(Gaelic, "The Skillful")*

□ **DANA** *(Scandinavian, "From Denmark")*.
DANICA.

□ **DANIELA** *(Hebrew, Fem. of Daniel, "God is my judge")*.
DANELLA, DANETTE, DANICE, DANITA, DANNIE, DANNY French: DANIELLE.

□ **DANIELLE** See DANIELA.

□ **DAPHNE** *(Greek, "Bay tree or laurel")*. The nymph of Greek mythology who escaped the god Apollo by changing into a laurel tree.

□ **DARA** *(Hebrew, "Home of compassion")*.

□ **DARBY** *(Irish, "Free man")*.
DARBIE.

□ **DARCIE** *(Old French, "The dark")*.
DARCY.

□ **DARLENE** *(Old English, "Little darling")*.
DARLA, DARLEEN, DARLINE.

□ **DAWN** *(Old English, "Daybreak")*.

□ **DEANNA** *(Old English, Fem. of Dean, "From the valley")*. See DENA, DIANA.

□ **DEBORAH** *(Hebrew, "The bee")*. The prophetess who helped free the Israelites.
DEB, DEBBIE, DEBBY. DEBORA, DEBRA.

□ **DEE** *(Gaelic, "Dark one")*. See DIANA, DEIRDRE, DELIA.

□ **DEIRDRE** *(Irish, "Wanderer")*. A legendary Irish heroine.
DEE, DEIRDRA, DIDI.

□ **DELFINE** *(Greek, "Delphinium flower")*. St. Delphine is the patron saint of maidens.
DELFINA, DELPHINA, DELPHINE.

□ **DELIA** *(Greek, "From the Isle of Delos")*.
DEE, DELINDA, DELIA, DELL, DELLA.

□ **DELILAH** *(Hebrew, "Gentle")*.
DALILA, DELILA, LILA.

□ **DELLA** See ADELAIDE, CORDELIA, DELIA.

□ **DELMA** *(Latin, Fem. of Delmer, "Of the sea")*.

□ **DELORES** See DOLORES.

□ **DENA** *(Hebrew, "Vindicated," Old English, "From the valley")*.
DEANA, DEANNA, DINA. (See DINAH).

□ **DENISE** *(Latin, Fem. of Denis, "Follower of Dionysus," the Greek god of wine)*. St. Denys is the patron saint of France.
DENNETTE, DENNY, DENYSE French: DENICE, DENYS.

□ **DIANA** *(Latin, "The divine")*. The Roman goddess of the moon and the hunt.
DEANNA, DEANNE, DEE, DENA, DIANNA, DIANNE, DIDI, DYAN, DYANNA French: DIANE.

□ **DIANE** See DIANA.

□ **DINAH** *(Hebrew, "Vindicated")*. The biblical daughter of Jacob and Leah.
DENA, DI, DINA.

□ **DIXIE** *(Latin, Dix, "The tenth")*.

□ **DODIE** See DORA, DOROTHY.

□ **DODY** See DORA, DOROTHY.

□ **DOLLIE, DOLLY** See DOROTHY.

□ **DOLORES** *(Spanish, "Sorrows")*. Referring to the sorrows of the Virgin Mary.
DELORA, DELORES, LOLA, LOLITA Spanish: DOLORITA.

□ **DOMINA** *(Latin, "Lady")*. From Domina comes Nadonna (my lady).

106

DOMELA, DONELLA, DONIA, MONA Italian: **DOMINA, DONNA**; Spanish: **DONA**.

☐ **DOMINICA** *(Latin, "belonging to the Lord")*.
French: **DOMINIQUE**; Italian: **DOMENICA**; Spanish: **DOMINGA**.

☐ **DONA** See DOMINA.

☐ **DONNA** See DOMINA.

☐ **DORA** *(Greek, "A gift")*.
DODIE, DODY, DORALIA, DORALICE, DORALIS, DORALYN, DOREEN, DORELIA, DORELLA, DORELLE, DORENA, DORETTA, DORETTE, DOREY, DORIE, DORITA, DORO, DORY German: **DORE**. (See DOROTHY, THEODORA).

☐ **DOREEN** *(Irish, "Sullen")*.
DORENE, DORI. (See DORA).

☐ **DORI** See DOREEN, DORIS.

☐ **DORINDA** *(Greek, "Beautiful")*.
DORENDA, DORI.

☐ **DORIS** *(Greek, "From the sea")*.
Eldoris was the Greek mythological mother of the sea nymphs.
DOREA, DORI, DORIA, DORICE, DORISA, DORISE, DORITA, DORRIS, DORY Greek: **ELDORIS**.

☐ **DOROTHY** *(Greek, "Gift of God")*. Originally Theodora, the name was reversed and became Dorothea. **DODIE, DODY, DOLLIE, DOLLY, DORA, DORLISS, DORATHEA, DORINDA, DORITA, DORTHEA, DORTHY, DORY, DOT, DOTTIE, DOTTY, THEA** French: **DORETTE, DOROTHEE**; German: **DORE, DOROTEA, DOROTHEA**; Polish: **DOROSIA**; Russian: **DARIJA, FEODORA**.

☐ **DOTTIE, DOTTY** See DOROTHY.

☐ **DYNA** *(Greek, "Power")*.

Most Popular "E" Name....
ELIZABETH

☐ **EARTHA** *(English, "Of the earth")*.
ERTHA.

☐ **EASTER** *(Old English, "Of the springtime")*.

☐ **ECHO** *(Greek, "Repeated sound")*. Spurned by Narcissus, Echo in the Greek myth languished until nothing was left but her voice.

☐ **EDA** See EDITH.

☐ **EDEN** *(Hebrew, "A place of delight")*.

☐ **EDITH** *(Old English, "Rich gift")*.

There were two English saints named Edith.

DITA, EDA, EDIE, EDITA Italian: **EDITA**.

□ **EDLYN** *(Old English, "Prosperous lady")*.

□ **EDNA** *(Hebrew, "Rejuvenation")*. The wife of Enoch in the Apocryphal Bible.
ED, EDDIE, EDDY.

□ **EFFIE** *(From the Greek, Euphemia, "Well spoken of")*.
EFFY, EUPHEMIA.

□ **ELAINE** See HELEN, ELEANORE.

□ **ELEANOR, ELEANORE** *(Old French, "Light")*. A form of Helen/ A 13th century English queen/The wife of F.D.R.
ELAINE, ELENORE, ELINOR, ELINORE, ELLA, ELLEN, ELLIE, ELLYN, ELNA, ELNORE, LEANOR, LENA, LENORA, LENORE, LEONORA, LEORA, NELL, NELLIE, NELLY, NORA Italian: **ELEONORA**; French: **ELEONORE**; Spanish: **LEANOR**; German/Danish: **ELEONORE.**

□ **ELENA** See HELEN.

□ **ELFRIDA** See ALFREDA.

□ **ELSIE, ELISSA** See ELIZABETH.

□ **ELIZABETH** *(Hebrew, "Oath of God")*. Four saints were named Elizabeth, one of them the mother of John the Baptist/One of the most popular names in England since the 16th Century Elizabeth I.
ELISABEH, ALISA, BESS, BESSIE, BESSY, BET, BETH, BETHIA, BETSY, BETT, BETTA, BETTE, BETTINA, BETTY, ELISABETH, ELISE, ELISSA, ELIZA, ELSBETH, ELSIE, ELYSE, LIBBY, LISA, LISABETH, LISBETH, LISA, LISE, LISETTA, LIZ, LIZA, LIZABETH, LIZBEBETH, LIZZETTA, LIZZIE, LIZZY French: **BABETTE, LISETTE**; Italian: **ELISA**; Spanish: **BELITA, ELISA, ISABEL, YSABEL**; German: **ILSE**; German/Dutch/Danish: **ELSA, ELSE**; Norwegian: **BESSE**; Swedish: **ELISABET**; Swiss: **BEBBA, BETHA**; Scotch: **ELSPETH**; Russian: **ELISAVETTA, LISENKA.**

□ **ELLA** *(Old English, "Elf")*.
ELLIE, ELLY.

□ **ELLEN** See HELEN.
ELLENE, ELLIE, ELLY.

□ **ELLICE** *(Hebrew, Fem. of Elias, "Jehovah is God")*

□ **ELRICA** See ALARICE.

□ **ELSA** *(Old German, "Noble")*.
ELSIE German: **ILSA** (See also **ELIZABETH**).

□ **ELVA** *(Old German, "Elf")*.
ELFIE, ELVIA, ELVIE.

□ **ELVINA** See ALVINA.

□ **ELVIRA** *(Latin, Albina, "White blonde")*.
ELVERA French: ELVIRE.

□ **ELYSIA** *(Greek, "Blissful")*.
ELSIE, ELISIA.

□ **EMILY** *(Teutonic, Fem. of Emil, "Industrious"; Latin, "Winsome")*.
AMALEA, AMALIA, AMELIA, AME-LIE, AMILIA, EM, EMALIRE, EMEL-DA, EMELEN, EMELINA, EMELINE, EMELITA, EMERA, EMILINE, EM-LYNNE, EMLYN, EMMELINE, EM-MIE, EMMY, MILLY French: EMILIE; Italian: EMILIA; German: AMALIE; Slavic: MILKA. (See AMELIA).

□ **EMMA** *(Old German "Nurse")*.
Queen Emma of the Netherlands.
EME, EMELINA, EMELINE, EME-LYNE, EMMALINE, EMMALYN, EM-MY Spanish: EMA.

□ **ERICA** *(Old Norse, Fem. of Eric, "The royal")*.
RICKIE, RICKY Swedish: ERIKA.

□ **ERIN** *(Irish, "From Ireland")*.
Erin or Eire is a literary name for Ireland.
ERINA.

□ **ERMA** See IRMA.

□ **ESMERALDA** *(Spanish, "A rare gem")*.
ESMA, ESME.

□ **ESTELLE** *(French, "A star")*.
ESSIE, ESTELE, ESTRELLA, STEL-LA Italian: ESTELLA; Spanish: ES-TRELITA. (See ESTHER).

□ **ESTHER** *(Persian, "A star")*.
Esther was the Persian name given to Hadassah, the Jewish captive who became queen of Persia and saved her people from destruction/Hester in Greek myth was the goddess of the hearth/The Latin *stella* means star.
ESSA, ESSIE, ESTELLINE, ESTRA, ESTRIE, ETTY, HESTER, HETTIE, HETTY, STELLA French: ESTELLE; Italian: ESTERRE; Spanish: ESTER.

□ **ETHEL** *(Old English, "Noble")*.
ETHELDA, ETHELEEN, ETHEL-INDA, ETHELINE, ETHELYN, ETH-YL, ETTIE.

□ **EUDORA** *(Greek, "Generous")*.
DORA French: EUDORE.

□ **EUGENIA** *(Greek, Fem. of Eugene, "Nobility")*. Eugenie was Empress of modern France and wife of Napoleon III./St. Eugenia was a 3rd Century Roman martyr.
GENE, GENIE French: EUGENIE.

☐ **EUNICE** *(Greek, "Happy victory")*. The Biblical mother of Timothy.

☐ **EUSTACIA** *(Latin, Fem. of Eustace, "Tranquil")*.
STACEY, STACIA, STACY.

☐ **EVA** See EVE.

☐ **EVANGELINE** *(Greek, "Bearer of good news")*.
EVA, EVANGELINA, EVE, VANGY.

☐ **EVE** *(Hebrew, "Life")*. The first woman and the mother of the human race.
EBA, EV, EVELINA, EVELINE, EVELYN, EVIE, EVLYN, EVY Italian/German: EVA; Spanish: EVITA; Russian: EVVA; Irish: EVELEEN; Greek: ZOE.

☐ **EVELYN** See EVE.

Most Popular
"F" Name.......
FRAN

☐ **FABIA** *(Latin, "Bean grower")*.
French: FABRIENNE; Italian: FABIOLA.

☐ **FAITH** *(Latin, "Belief in God")*. One of the Puritan "virtue" names.
FAY. (See FAY).

☐ **FANNY** See FRANCES.

☐ **FAY** *(Old French, "Fairy")*.
FAYE, FAYETTE. See FAITH.

☐ **FELICIA** *(Latin, Fem. of Felix, "Happy")*.
FELICIANA, FELICITY, FELITA French: FELICITE, FELISE; Italian: FELICE, FELICITA.

☐ **FERN** *(Old English, "A fern")*.

☐ **FLORA** *(Latin, "A flower")*. The Roman goddess of spring and flowers.
FLO, FLOR, FLORIS, FLORRIE French: FLORE; Italian: FIORA.

☐ **FLORENCE** *(Latin, "Blooming," "Flourishing")*. Florence in Italy was named for Flora, the Roman goddess of flowering plants/Seven saints were named Florence/Florence Nightengale was the first battlefield nurse.
FLO, FLORELLA, FLORENDA, FLORET, FLORETTE, FLORETTA, FLORI, FLORIA, FLORIDA, FLORIDE, FLORIE, FLORINA, FLORINE, FLORINDA, FLORRIE, FLORRY, FLOSS, FLOSSIE, FLOYCE Italian: FIORENZA; Spanish: FLORENCIA, FLORENCITA; German: FLORENTIA.

☐ **FRAN** See FRANCES.

☐ **FRANCES** *(Latin, "The free one," or "Of France")*. The name of many male and female saints.
FAN, FANIA, FANNIE, FANNY, FRAN,

FRANCI, FRANCIA, FRANCI, FRAN-
CIE, FRANCINE, FRANKIE, FRANKY,
FRANNY French: FANCHETTE, FAN-
CHON, FRANCOISE; Italian: FRAN-
CESCA, CECCA, CECCARELLA, CEC-
CINA; Spanish: FRANCISCA; Dutch:
FRANCINA, FRANSJE; German:
FRANZISKA, FRANZE; Polish: FRAN-
CISZKA; Russian: FRANZISKA.

☐ **FREDA** *(German, "Peace")*.
FRIDA German: FRIEDA.

☐ **FREDERICA** *(Old German,
Fem. of Frederick, "Peaceful ruler")*.
Frederika was a Queen of Greece.
FREDERIKA, FREDDIE, FREDDY,
RICA, RICKI, RICKIE Italian/Span-
ish: FEDERICA; German: FRITZE,
RIKE.

☐ **FRIEDA** See FREDA.

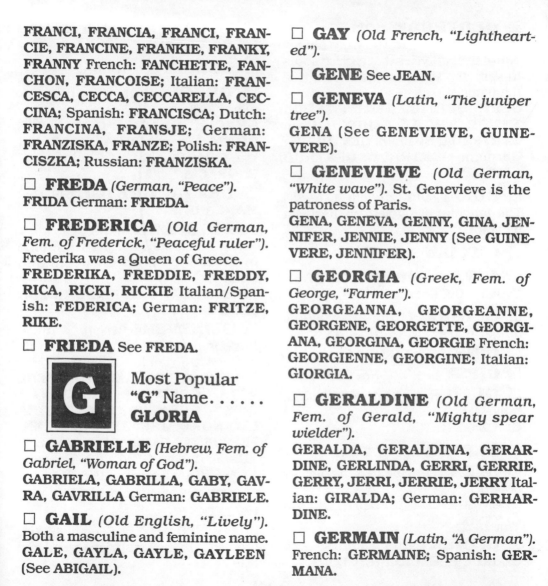

Most Popular
"G" Name......
GLORIA

☐ **GABRIELLE** *(Hebrew, Fem. of
Gabriel, "Woman of God")*.
GABRIELA, GABRILLA, GABY, GAV-
RA, GAVRILLA German: GABRIELE.

☐ **GAIL** *(Old English, "Lively")*.
Both a masculine and feminine name.
GALE, GAYLA, GAYLE, GAYLEEN
(See ABIGAIL).

☐ **GAY** *(Old French, "Lightheart-
ed")*.

☐ **GENE** See JEAN.

☐ **GENEVA** *(Latin, "The juniper
tree")*.
GENA (See GENEVIEVE, GUINE-
VERE).

☐ **GENEVIEVE** *(Old German,
"White wave")*. St. Genevieve is the
patroness of Paris.
GENA, GENEVA, GENNY, GINA, JEN-
NIFER, JENNIE, JENNY (See GUINE-
VERE, JENNIFER).

☐ **GEORGIA** *(Greek, Fem. of
George, "Farmer")*.
GEORGEANNA, GEORGEANNE,
GEORGENE, GEORGETTE, GEORGI-
ANA, GEORGINA, GEORGIE French:
GEORGIENNE, GEORGINE; Italian:
GIORGIA.

☐ **GERALDINE** *(Old German,
Fem. of Gerald, "Mighty spear
wielder")*.
GERALDA, GERALDINA, GERAR-
DINE, GERLINDA, GERRI, GERRIE,
GERRY, JERRI, JERRIE, JERRY Ital-
ian: GIRALDA; German: GERHAR-
DINE.

☐ **GERMAIN** *(Latin, "A German")*.
French: GERMAINE; Spanish: GER-
MANA.

☐ **GERTRUDE** *(Old German, "Spear maiden")*. In Norse mythology one of the Valkyries that carried souls to Valhalla/Three saints have borne the name.
GERT, GERTIE, GERTY, TRUDA, TRUDE, TRUDI, TRUDY Italian: GERTRUDA; Spanish: GERTRUDIS; German: GERTRAUD, GERTRUD, GERTRUT.

☐ **GILDA** *(Old English, "Gilded")*. The daughter of Rigoletto in the opera by Verdi.

☐ **GILLIAN** See JULIA.

☐ **GINA** See ANGELINA, GENE-VIEVE, REGINA.

☐ **GINGER** *(Latin, "The yellow ginger flower")*. See VIRGINIA.

☐ **GINNY** See VIRGINIA.

☐ **GIPSY** See GITANA, GYPSY.

☐ **GLADYS** *(Latin, "Gladiolus,' "sword")*.
GLAD, GLADINE.

☐ **GLENDA** See GLENNA.

☐ **GLENNA** *(Irish, "Of the glen or valley")*.
GLENDA, GLENNIS, GLYN, GLYNIS, GLYNNIE.

☐ **GLORIA** *(Latin, "Glory")*.
GLORIANA, GLORIANE, GLORY.

☐ **GOLDA** *(Old English, "Gold")*. GILDA, GOLDIE.

☐ **GOLDIE** See GOLDA.

☐ **GRACE** *(Latin, "Graceful," "Thanks")*.
GRACIA, GRACIE, GRACIENNE, GRAYCE French: GRAZIELLE; Italian: GRAZIA, GRAZIOSA; Spanish: ENGRACIA.

☐ **GRETA, GRETCHEN** See MARGARET.

☐ **GRISELDA** *(Old German, "Gray battle maiden")*. The heroine in stories by both Bocaccio and Chaucer.
CHRISELDA, GRIZELDA, SELDA, ZELDA.

☐ **GUINEVERE** *(Welsh, "White or fair complected")*. King Arthur's wife in the Arthurian legends.
GAYNOR, GENAVIE, GENEVA, GENE-VION, GENIVEVE, GUENEVER, GWEN, GUENEVERE, GWENORA, GWENORE, JEN, JENNIE, JENNI-FER, JENNY, VANORA French: GENE-VIEVE; Italian: GENEVRA; Russian: ZENEVIEVA; Scotch: GINEVRA.

☐ **GWEN** See GUINEVERE and GWENDOLYN.

☐ **GWENDOLYN** *(Welsh, "White browed")*. In the Arthurian legend, the wife of Merlin.

GUENNA, GWEN, GWENDA, GWEN-
NIE, GWENDOLEN, GWYN, GWYN-
ETH, WENDY.

□ **GWYN** *(Welsh, "White or fair")*.
GWEN, WENDY, WYNETTE, WYNNE
(See GWENDOLYN).

□ **GYPSY** *(Old English, Gipryan,
"A gypsy, a wanderer, or from Egypt")*.
GIPSY.

Most Popular
"H" Name......
HEATHER

□ **HALIMEDA** *(Greek, "Thinking
of the sea")*.
HALLEY.

□ **HALLIE** See HALIMEDA, HAR-
RIET, HARELDA.

□ **HANA** *(Japanese, "Flower")*.

□ **HANNAH** *(Hebrew, "Graceful")*.
The Biblical Hannah was the mother
of the prophet Samuel. See ANN

□ **HAPPY** See HEPZIBETH.

□ **HARRIET** *(Old French, Fem. of
Hatty, "Head of the estate")*.
HARRIETTA, HARRIETTE, HATTIE,
HATTY (See HENRIETTA).

□ **HATTIE** See HENRIETTA and
HARRIET.

□ **HAZEL** *(Old English, "Hazel
tree")*. The hazel branch was the emblem of authority in parts of ancient
Europe.

□ **HEATHER** *(Middle English,
"The heath," "Heather")*. The heaths
of England and Scotland were named
for the flowering shrubs of the same
name.

□ **HEDDA** *(Old German, "Strife")*.
See HEDWIG.

□ **HEDY** *(Greek, "Sweet")*.

□ **HEIDI** From the German name
ADELHEID. See ADELAIDE.

□ **HELEN** *(Greek, "Light")*. An ancient goddess in Greek and Roman
mythology/ St. Helena, was the mother of Emperor Constantine/ In the
Illiad, Helen of Troy possessed the
beautiful face "that launched 1000
ships"/ Helen is the symbol of the
eternal woman.

AILENE, ELAINE, ELANE, ELEAN-
ORE, ELENA, ELINORE, ELLA,
ELENE, ELLEN, ELLENE, ELLIE,
ELLETTE, ELLY, ELLYN, HELAINE,
HELANA, HELENE, ILENE, LANA,
LENA, LINA, LENORA, LENORE,
LEONORE, LEORA, LORA, LORENE,
NELL, NELLIE, NELLY, NORA Greek:

113

HELENE; Latin: **HELENA**; French: **ELAINE, HELENE**; Italian: **ELENA, ELEONORA, LEONORA**; Spanish: **ELENA**; German: **ELEONORE, HELENA, LENORE, LEONORE**; Hungarian: **ILONA**; Polish: **HALINA**; Slavic: **LENKA**; Russian: **GALINA**; Irish: **AILEEN, AILLEEN, ALLIE, EILEEN**; Scotch: **ELLEN**.

☐ **HELGA** (Old German, "Religious," "Holy"). See **OLGA**.

☐ **HELICE** (Greek, "Spiral").

☐ **HELOISE** See **LOUISE**.

☐ **HENRIETTA** (French, "Mistress of the estate").
ENRICA, ETTA, ETTIE, HARRIET, HARRIOTT, HATTIE, HATTY, HETTIE, HETTY, NETTIE, YETTA French: **HENRIETTE**; Italian: **ENRICHETTA**; Spanish: **ENRIQUETA**; Dutch: **HENDRIKA**; Swedish: **HENRIKA**.

☐ **HEPZIBETH** (Hebrew, "She is my delight").
HAPPY, HEPSY, HEP.

☐ **HERMIONE** (Greek, Fem. of Greek god Heimes, "Of the earth"). The daughter of Helen of Troy in the Greek myths.
ERMA, HERMIA, HERMINA, HERMINE (See **ARMINA**).

☐ **HESTER** (Greek, "Star"). Heroine of Hawthorne's novel, *The Scarlet Letter*.
HETTIE, HETTY.

☐ **HILARY** (Greek, "Cheerful"). French: **HILARIA**; Russian: **ILARIA**.

☐ **HILDA** (Old German, "Battle maid"). In Norse mythology Hilda was one of the Valkyrs that carried souls to Valhalla.
HILDE, HILDIE, HILDY (See **HILDE-GARDE**).

☐ **HOLLY** (Old English, "Holly tree," "Holy"). The holly wreath was used in ancient England as a decoration at Christmas time to bring good luck.

☐ **HONEY** (Old English, "Sweet"). See **HONORA** or **HONORIA**.

☐ **HOPE** (Old English, "Hope"). One of the Puritan "virtue" names.

I Most Popular "I" Name . . . . **ILENE**

☐ **IDA** (Old German, "Youthful labor,"/ Old English, "Rich"). In Greek mythology, Mount Ida was favored by the gods.
IDALIA, IDALINA, IDALINE German: **IDELLE, IDETTE.**

☐ **ILANA** (Hebrew, "Stout tree").

☐ **ILEANA** *(Greek, "From the city of Troy").*

☐ **ILENE** See HELEN.

☐ **IMOGENE** *(Latin, "An image").* EMOGENE, IMELDA German: **IMAGINA**.

☐ **INA** *(Latin).* Ina is an independent name that began as a suffix used in the Spanish and Italian male names to make them feminine.

☐ **INGRID** *(Old Norse, "Ing's daughter").* Ing was the old Norse god of prosperity and fertility. INGA, INGAR, INGE.

☐ **IONA** *(Greek, "Violet colored stone").*

☐ **IRENE** *(Greek, "Peace").* In Greek mythology Eirene was the goddess of peace/ Of four St. Irenes, one was the Empress of Constantinople/ Irene Curie shared the 1933 Nobel Prize for chemistry. IRENA, IRINA, RENE, RENA.

☐ **IRIS** *(Greek, "A rainbow").* The goddess of the rainbow in Greek mythology.

☐ **IRMA** *(Old German, "Noble person").* ERMA (See ARMINA).

☐ **ISABEL** *(Spanish, "Consecrated to God").* Of several Queens of Spain named Isabel, one sponsored Columbus. BEL, BELL, BELLA, BELLE, ISA, ISABELLE French: ISABEAU; Italian: ISABELLA; Spanish: YSABEL; Scottish: ISOBEL, TIBBIE; Irish: ISHBEL.

☐ **ISADORA** *(Greek, Fem of Isidore, "Gift of Isis").* Isis was the Egyptian goddess of the Nile and fertility.

☐ **ISIS** *(Egyptian, "The supreme goddess").* See ISADORA.

☐ **IVY** *(Greek, "The ivy plant").* To the ancient Greeks, ivy was sacred to Bacchus the god of wine/ The English adopted Ivy as a female name.

J Most Popular "J" Name....... **JENNIFER**

☐ **JACKIE** See JACQUELINE, JACOBA.

☐ **JACOBA** *(Hebrew, Fem. of Jacob, "Supplanter").* JACKIE, JACKY, JACOBINA, JACOBINE.

☐ **JACQUELINE** *(French, Fem of the Hebrew Jacob and the French*

Jacques).

JACALYN, JACKIE, JACKY, JACLYN, JACQUELYN, JACOBINA, JACQUE-NETTA, JACQUENETTE, JACQUET-TA, JACQUETTE German: JAKO-BINE; Russian: JACOVINA, ZAKE-LINA.

□ **JADE** *(Spanish, "Jade stone").*
Spani sh: JADA.

□ **JAEL** *(Hebrew, "Spreader of light").*

□ **JAMIE** *(Fem. of James).*
JAMESINA.

□ **JAN** See JANE.

□ **JANE** *(Hebrew, "God is gra-cious").* Along with Jean and Joanne, Jane is a familiar feminine form of John/ Among the saints who have borne this name in one of its forms are Jeanne d'Arc and Giovanna of Naples.
GENE, GIANNA, JAN, JANEL, JAN-ELLA, JANELLE, JANET, JANETTE, JANEY, JANIA, JANICE, JANIE, JANINA, JANINE, JANIS, JANNA, JANOT, JANY, JEAN, JEANIE, JEAN-NINE, JENNICE, JENNIE, JINNY, JENNETA, JO, JOAN, JOANIE, JOAN-NA, JOANNE, JOEANNA, JOEANNE, JOHANNA, JOHNETTE, JONETTE, JONI, JONNIE French: JEANNE, JEANNETTE; Italian: GIANINA, GIO-VANNA; Spanish: JUANA, JUANITA, NITA; German: JOHANNA, JOHANNE; Irish: SHEENA, SHENA; Scotch: JEN-NY, JINNY; Russian: VANIA, ZANETA.

□ **JANET** See JANE.

□ **JANICE** See JANE.

□ **JEAN** See JANE.

□ **JEANNETTE** See JANE.

□ **JENNIFER** See GENEVIEVE.

□ **JENNY** See GENEVIEVE, GUI-NEVERE, JANE.

□ **JERONIMA** *(Greek, Fem, of Je-rome, "Holy name").*
JERRIE, JERRY.

□ **JERRI, JERRIE, JERRY** See GERALDINE, JERONIMA, JERUSHA.

□ **JERUSHA** *(Hebrew, "The mar-ried," "Possessed").*
JERRY, JERUSA, JERUSHY

□ **JESSICA** *(Hebrew, Fem. of Jesse, "Wealthy one").*
JESS, JESSALYN, JESSIE, JESSLYN, JESSY.

□ **JESSIE, JESSY** See JESSI-CA.

□ **JILL** See JULIA, GILLIAN.

□ **JINNY** See JANE, VERGINIA.

☐ **JO** Short for names beginning with "Jo."

☐ **JOAN** See JANE.

☐ **JOANNA, JOANNE** See JANE.

☐ **JOCELYN** *(Old English, "The just")*. ✓
JOCELIN, JOCELINE, JOSCELIND, JOSCELINE (See JOYCE, JUSTINE).

☐ **JODY** See JUDITH.

☐ **JOELLE** *(Hebrew, Fem. of Joel, "The Lord is willing")*.
JOELA, JOELLA.

☐ **JOLENE** See JOSEPHINE.

☐ **JORDANA** *(Hebrew, Fem. of Jordan, "The decending")*.

☐ **JOSEPHINE** *(Hebrew, Fem. of Joseph, "He shall add")*. Napoleon's wife Josephine, Empress of France.
JO, JOETTE, JOEY, JOLENE, JOSE-PHINE, JOSETTE, JOSIE French: FIFI, FIFINE, JOSEPHE; Italian: GIU-SEPPINA; Spanish: JOSEFA, JOSE-FINA; German: JOSEPHA.

☐ **JOY** *(Latin, "Joyful")*.
JOYANA, JOYCE, JOYCELIN, JOYCE-LYN (See JACELYN).

☐ **JOYCE** See JOY.

☐ **JUDITH** *(Hebrew, Fem. of Judah, "Praised")*. The beautiful woman of the Apocrypha who saved her village by slaying Holofernes.
JODI, JODIE, JODY, JUDIE, JUDY French: JUDITHE; Italian: GIUDITTA; German: JUDITHA; Irish: SIOBHAN.

☑ **JULIA** *(Latin, Fem. of Julius, "Youthful")*. Juliana was Queen of the Netherlands/ The month of July was named after Julius Caesar.
GILLIAN, GILLIE, JILL, JOLETTA, JULETTE, JULY, JULIE, JULIET, JU-LINA, JULINE French: JULIANE, JU-LIE, JULIENNE, JULIETTE; Spanish: JULIANA, JULIETTA; Italian: GIULIA, GIULIETTA; German: JULIE; Russian: JULIJA; Irish: SILE.

☐ **JUNE** *(Latin, Fem. of Junius, "June")*.
JUNETH, JUNETTE, JUNIA, JUNIA-TA, JUNIE, JUNINA, JUNINE, JUNITA.

K
Most Popular "K" Name . . .
KRISTIN

☐ **KALI** *(Sanskrit, "Universal energy")*.

☐ **KAMA** *(Hindu, "Love")*.

☐ **KAMEKO** *(Japanese, "The tortoise")*.

117

☐ **KAREN** See KATHERINE.

☐ **KARLA** See CHARLOTTE.

☐ **KASMIRA** *(Slavic, Fem. of Casimir, "Commands peace").*
KASS, KASEY, KASSY.

✗ ☑ **KATE** See CATHERINE.

✓ ☑ **KATHERINE** See CATHERINE.

☐ **KAY** See CATHERINE.

☐ **KEIKO** *(Japanese, "Adored").*

✓ ☑ **KELLY** *(Irish, "Warrior maid").*

☐ **KELSEY** *(Old Norse, "From the island refuge").*

☐ **KENDRA** *(Old English, "Knowing").*

☐ **KERRY** See CATHERINE.

☐ **KIM** *(Old English, "Ruler").*

☐ **KIMBERLY** *(Old English, "From the rulers' meadow").*
KIM.

✓ ☑ **KRISTIN** See CHRISTINE.
Christa

Most Popular
"L" Name. . . .
LAURA

☐ **LANA** See HELEN and ALANNA.

☐ **LALITA** *(Sanskrit, "Pleasant").*

☐ **LANI** *(Hawaiian, "Sky").*

☐ **LARA** *(Latin, "Shining," "Famous one").*

☐ **LARAINE** *(Latin, "Sea bird").*
LARINA, LARINE See LORRAINE.

☐ **LARISSA** *(Latin, "Cheerful").*
LACEY.

☐ **LAURA** *(Latin, Fem. of Lawrence, "The laurel").*
LAUREEN, LAUREL, LAURELLA, LAUREN, LAURENA, LAURELLE, LAURETTA, LAURICE, LAURINDA, LAWRENA, LORA, LORALIE, LORELLE, LOREN, LORENA, LORETTA, LORETTE, LORI, LORINDA, LORITA, LORNA, LORRIE, LORRY Latin: LAURENTIA; French: LAURE, LAURETTE, LOULOU; Italian: LORENZA.

☐ **LAUREN** See LAURA.

☐ **LAVERNE** *(Latin, Vernis, "Springlike").*

☐ **LAVINIA** *(Latin, "Purified").*
LAVINA, LAVINE, LAVETTA, LAVETTE.

☐ **LEAH** *(Hebrew, "The weary one").*
Leah was the wife of Jacob.
LEE French: LEA; Italian: LIA.

118

☐ **LEALA** *(Old French, "Faithful")*. LEALIA, LEALIE, LELAH, LOYALE, LOYOLA.

☐ **LEANA** See LIANA.

☐ **LEE** *(Old English, Leah, "From the meadow")*. LEANN, LEANNA, LEIGH. (See LEAH).

☐ **LEIGH** See LEE.

☐ **LEILA** *(Arabic, "Dark as night")*. The lover of Majnum in the Persian legend. LAYLA, LILA Arabic: LEILAH.

☐ **LEILANI** *(Hawaiian, "Heavenly flower")*.

☐ **LELIA** *(French/Latin, "Lily")*. LAELIA, LELA See LILLIAN.

☐ **LENA** *(Latin, "Temptress")*. See LENIS, HELEN, MADALINE, MAGDELENA.

☐ **LENORE** See HELEN.

☐ **LEORA** See ELEANOR.

☐ **LEONA** *(Latin, Fem. of Leo, "Lion")*. LEOLA, LEOLINE, LEOLYN, LEONE, LEONELLA, LEONELLE French: LEONIE; Spanish: LEOCADIA.

☐ **LESLIE** *(Scotch, "From the gray stronghold")*. LESLEY, LESLY.

☐ **LETITIA** *(Latin, "Joy")*. LETICIA, LETTICE, LETTIE, LETTY, TISH, TISHA.

☐ **LEVINA** *(Middle English, "The flash," "Lightning")*.

☐ **LEYA** *(Spanish 'Loyalty")*.

☐ **LILA** See LEILA.

☐ **LILITH** *(Arabic, 'Belonging to the night")*. In Semitic mythology the first wife of Adam/ She was also the witch in Goethe's *Faust*.

☐ **LILLIAN** *(Latin, "A lily, flower")*. The lily was a Christian symbol of purity. LIL, LILA, LILIAH, LILAS, LILI, LILIA, LILIAN, LILIAS, LILIE, LILY, LILLY, LILYAN Latin: LILLIS.

☐ **LINA** Terminal ending of diminutives, such as Carolina, Adeline, Madeline, etc.

☐ **LINDA** *(Spanish, "Beautiful")*. LINDY, LYNDA.

☐ **LINDSEY** *(Old English, "The linden tree island")*.

☐ **LINETTE** *(Old French, "The linnet bird")*. In the Arthurian legends, Lynette was the lover of Gareth. LANETTE, LINET, LINETTA, LYNETTE See LYNN.

☐ **LISA** See ELIZABETH.

☐ **LIVIA** *(Latin, "Frivolous")*. Livia was the first empress of Rome. See OLIVE.

☐ **LOIS** See LOUISE.

☐ **LOLA** See DOLORES.

☐ **LOLITA** See DOLORES.

☐ **LONA** *(Middle English, "Lone")*.

☐ **LORA** See LAURA.

☐ **LORELEI** *(German, "Alluring")*. See LURLINE.

☐ **LORETTA** See LAURA.

☐ **LORINDA** See LAURA.

☐ **LORRAINE** (French, "From Lorraine"). Loraine is a province in France.
LORAINE.

☐ **LOTTIE** See CHARLOTTE.

☐ **LOUISE** *(Old German, "Famous warrior")*. A name that has many forms, including **HELOISE, ELOISE, ALISON,** and **LOUELLA.**
ALISON, ALLIE, ALLISON, ALOISA, ALOYSIA, ELOISA, ELOISE, HELOISA, LOIS, LOU, LOUELLA, LOUISA, LOUISSETTA, LOUISETTE, LOUISINE, LOULA, LULU French: ALOYSE, HELOISE; Italian/Spanish: LUISA; German: LUISE; Swedish: LOVISA; Scotch: ALISON; Polish: LUANA, LUDOISIA, LUDVICA.

☐ **LUANA** *(Old German, "Graceful warrior")*.
LOUANNA, LUANE, LUANN.

☐ **LUCILLE** See LUCY.

☐ **LUCINDA** See LUCY, CINDY.

☐ **LUCRETIA** *(Latin, "Rich rewards")*.
French: LUCRECE; Italian: LUCREZIA; Spanish: LUCRECIA.

☐ **LUCY** *(Latin, Fem. of LUCIUS, "Light")*. In Roman mythology, Lucina was the goddess of both the moon and childbirth/ Three saints bear this name, among them St. Lucia, the patroness of Italy.
CINDY, LOU, LU, LUCETTE, LUCIDA, LUCIANA, LUCILE, LUCILIA, LUCINA, LUCINDA, LULA, LULITA, LULU French: LUCIE, LUCIENNE, LUCILLE; Italian: LUCIA; Spanish: LUZ.

☐ **LUDMILLA** *(Slavic, "Loved by the people")*.

☐ **LUNA** *(Latin, "The moon")*.

☐ **LURLINE** *(German, "Alluring")*.
LURA, LURAH, LURANA, LUREL, LURENA, LURETTA, LURETTE, LURILLA, LURLEEN, LURLENE German: LORELEI.

☐ **LYDIA** *(Greek, "From Lydia")*. An ancient country in Asia Minor noted for its beautiful women and its king, Midas.
LIDDY.

☐ **LYNN** *(Old English, "A waterfall")*.
LYNELLE, LYNETTE.

☐ **LYSANDRA** *(Greek, "Liberator")*.
LYSIA.

☐ **LYRA** *(Greek, "The harp")*.

M

Most Popular "M" Name...
MICHELLE

☐ **MABEL** *(Latin, "The amiable," "Lovable")*. A form of the name Amabel, one of the *Ami* or "joy" names.
MABELLE, MABLE, MAYBELLE.

☐ **MACKENZIE** *(Irish, "Son of the wise leader")*.

☐ **MADELINE** *(Greek, "Woman of Magdala")*. Magda, a town on the Sea of Galilee, was the birthplace of St. Mary of Magdalene.
LENA, LINA, MADA, MADDY, MADALENE, MADEL, MADELLA, MADELLE, MADELAINE, MADLEN, MAGDALA, MAGDALEN, MAGDALENE, MALENA, MADGE, MALA, MALINA, MARLEEN, MARLENA, MARLENE, MARLINE, MARLYN, MAUD French: MADELEINE, MADELON, MAGDELAINE; Italian: MADDALENA; Spanish: MADELENA, MAGDELENA; Danish: MAGLI, MALIN, MALINA; German: MADLEN, MADY, MAGDALENE; Polish: MAGDELINA; Russian: MADELINA.

☐ **MADGE** See MADELINE, MARGARET.

☐ **MAE** See MARY, MAY.

☐ **MAGDALENE** See MADELINE.

☐ **MAGGIE** See MARGARET.

☐ **MALINDA** *(Greek, "Gentle")*.
MALINA.

☐ **MALVINA** *(Gaelic, Fem. of Melvin, "Chieftain")*. A heroine of ancient Irish myths.
MAL, MALVA, MALVIE, MALVINIA, MELVA, MELVIE, MELVINA, MELVINE French: MALVINE.

☐ **MAMIE** See MARY.

☐ **MANDY** See AMANDA.

☐ **MARA** See MARY.

☐ **MARCELLA** *(Latin, "Warlike," "Of Mars")*.
MARCELLE, MARCELLINA, MARCELLINE, MARCIE, MARCY Spanish: MARCELA (See MARCIA).

☐ **MARCIA** (Latin, "Warlike").
MARCELENA, MARCELIA, MAR-CELLA, MARCELLINE, MARCERITA, MARCHETA, MARCIE, MARCY, MAR-KITA, MARSHA Italian: MARZIA.

☐ **MARCIE** See MARCIA.

☐ **MARELDA** (Old German, "Battle maid").
MARILDA.

☑ **MARGARET** (Latin, "A pearl").
In addition to the patron saint of Scotland, there were three other saints Margaret/ A traditional name of European royalty/ It is also a "flower" name (the daisy-French, "mar guerite").
GRETA, MADGE, MAG, MAGGIE, MAGGY, MARGA, MARGALO, MAR-GARETA, MARGARETE, MARGAR-ETHE, MARGARETTA, MARGAR-ETTE, MARGE, MARGERY, MARGET, MARGETTE, MARGIE, MARGIT, MARGO, MARGUERITA, MARGY, MARJIE, MARJORY, MARKETA, MEGAN, MEGGI, META, PEG, PE-GEEN, PEGGIE, PEGGY, RITA French: MARGOT, MARGUERITE; Italian: MARGHERITA; Spanish: MARGAR-ITA, RITA; Danish: MARET, MAR-GARETE; German: GRETCHEN, GRETEL, GRETTA, MARGHET; Slav-ic: MARJARITA, MARJETA: Irish: MEGHAN; Scotch: MAISIE, MAR-JORIE, MEG.

☐ **MARGOT** See MARGARET.

☐ **MARIA, MARIE** See MARY.

☐ **MARIAN** See MARY.

☐ **MARIE** See MARY.

☐ **MARILYN** See MARY, MERRY.

☐ **MARINA** (Latin, "Of the sea").
MARNA, MARNI, MEARA, MERIS.

☐ **MARIS** (Latin, "Of the sea").
MARISA, MARISSA, MERIS See MARINA.

☐ **MARJORIE** See MARGARET.

☐ **MARLA** See MARY.

☐ **MARLENE** See MADELINE.

☐ **MARLO** See MARY.

☐ **MARNA** See MARINA.

☐ **MARNI** See MARINA.

☐ **MARSHA** See MARCIA.

☐ **MARTHA** (Aramaic, "Lady").
The biblical sister of Mary Magdalen and Lazarus/ The patron saint of homemakers.
MART, MARTELLA, MARTELLE, MARTHENA, MARTIE, MARTITA, MARTY, MATTIE, MATTY French/ German: MARTHE; Italian/Spanish: MARTA; Russian: MARFA.

☐ **MARTINA** *(Latin, "Warlike one")*.
MARTA, MARTIE, TINA French: MARTINE.

☐ **MARY** *(Hebrew, "Bitter")*. First mentioned in the Bible as Marah, meaning myrrh, the bitter ointment: "Call me Marah, the bitter, for the almighty hath dealt very bitterly with me"/ Mary became the most common Christian female name in the world, in honor of the Virgin Mary, mother of Jesus/ The oldest form of the name is actually Miriam, the sister of Moses.
MAIRE, MAME, MAMIE, MARA, MARALINE, MARELLA, MARELLE, MARETTA, MARETTE, MARI, MARIAN, MARIANA, MARYANN, MARIANNA, MARIANNE, MARCIA, MARICE, MARIEL, MARIETTA, MARIETTE, MARILINE, MARILLA, MARILYN, MARINKA, MARION, MARISKA, MARITE, MARJA, MARLA, MARLO, MARYA MARYANN, MARYLOU, MARYRUTH, MARYSIA, MATELLE, MAY, MAURENE, MAURITA, MOLL, MOLLY, MURIEL, MURIELLE, POLLY See POLLYANNA French: MANETTE, MANON, MARIE; Irish: MAURA, MAUREEN, MOIRA, MOYA; Spanish: MARIA, MARITA; Polish: MARYA See MIRIAM.

☐ **MATILDA** *(Old German, "Mighty battlemaid")*. A German name introduced to England by the wife of William the Conqueror.
MATHILDA, MATTY, MAUD, MAUDIE, TILDA, TILLY Italian: MATELDA; German/French: MATHILDE; Spanish: MATILDE.

☐ **MAUREEN** See MARY.

☐ **MAVIS** *(French: 'Thrush")*.

☐ **MAXINE** *(Latin, Fem. of Max, "Maximum," "Greatest")*. Popularized in France.
MAX, MAXIE French: MAXIME.

☐ **MAY** *(Latin, Maia, "The great")*. Maia was the Roman goddess of spring and the wife of Vulcan.
MAE, MAI.

☐ **MEARA** *(Irish, "Mirth")*.

☐ **MEG** See MARGARET.

☑ **MEGAN** *(Greek, Megas, "Mighty")*. The Irish use Meghan as a form of Margaret.
MEG, MEGHAN.

☑ **MELANIE** *(Greek, "The dark")*. A Greek goddess who wore black all winter.
MELAIN, MELAINA, MELANIA, MELLIE.

☐ **MELINA** *(Latin, "Yellow colored")*.

☐ **MELINDA** *(Greek, "Gentle")*.
LINDA, LINDY, MALINA, MALINDA, MANDY.

✓ ☑ **MELISSA** *(Greek, "Honey," "Honey bee")*. In Greek mythology, Melissa taught the world to use honey.
LISSA, MELESSA, MELICENT, MELISA, MELISE, MELISENDRA, MELITA, MELLETA, MELLIE, MELLY, MILICENT, MILLI, MILLICENT, MILLISENT, MILLIE, MILLY, MISSY French: MELISANDE, MELISSE, MELUSINE; Spanish: MELISENDA.

☐ **MELODIE** *(Greek, "A song")*.
MELODY Greek: MELOSA.

☐ **MERCY** *(Latin, "Pity," "Mercy")*. A religious name popular in Latin countries in honor of "Our Lady of Mercy".
Italian: MERCEDE; Spanish: MERCEDES.

☐ **MEREDITH** *(Welsh, "Protector of the sea")*.
MEREDEE, MERRY.

☐ **MERLE** *(Latin, "Blackbird")*.
MERLA, MERLINA, MERLINE, MERYL, MYRLE, MYRLENE.

☐ **MERNA** See MORNA, MYRNA.

☐ **MERRY** See MEREDITH.

☐ **MERYL** See MERLE.

☐ **MIA** *(Italian, "Mine")*.

☐ **MICHAELA** *(Hebrew, Fem. of Michael, "Who is like God")*.
MICHAEL, MICHELINA, MICHELINE, MICKIE French: MICHELLE; Italian: MICHAELE, MICHAELLA; Spanish: MIGUELA, MIGUELITA; German: MICHAELINE; Russian: MIKELINA.

☐ **MICHELLE** See MICHAELA.

☐ **MILA** *(Italian, "The loveable")*.
MILANA.

☐ **MILDRED** *(Old English, "Mild power")*.
MIL, MILDRID, MILLIE, MILLY.

☐ **MILICENT** *(Old German, "Industrious")*.
MELICENT, MIL, MILLICENT, MILLIE MILLY French: MELISANDE; Spanish: MELISENDA (See MELISSA).

☐ **MILLIE, MILLY** See CAMILLA, EMILY, MELISSA, MILDRED, MILICENT.

☐ **MIMI** See MIRIAM.

☐ **MINERVA** *(Latin, "Wisdom")*.
MINNY.

☐ **MINNA** *(Old German, "Love")*.
MINA, MINDA, MINDY, MINETTA, MINNIE German: MINETTE, MINNE.

☐ **MINNIE** *(Scottish, "Mother")*
See MINERVA, MINNA.

☐ **MIRA** *(Latin, "Wonderful")*. MIRELLE, MYRA.

☐ **MIRANDA** *(Latin, "Admirable")*. "Admired Mirande!" Shakespeare, *The Tempest*. MYRA.

☐ **MIRIAM** *(Hebrew, Miryam, "Bitter")*. MIMI, MITZI (See MARY).

☐ **MIRNA** See MYRNA.

☐ **MISSY** See MELISSA.

☐ **MITZI** See MIRIAM.

☐ **MOLLY** See MARY.

☐ **MONA** *(Italian, "My lady")*.

☐ **MONICA** *(Latin, "The advisor")*. St. Monica was the mother of St. Augustine.

☐ **MORNA** *(Celtic, "Soft," "Gentle")*. MERNA, MOINA, MOYNA Celtic: MUIRNE (See MYRNA).

☐ **MURIEL** *(Greek, "Myrrh")*. MERIAL, MERIEL, MERRIL, MERRILLA (See MARY).

☐ **MYRA** *(Greek, "Abundance")*.

☐ **MYRNA** *(Irish, "Polite")*. MERNA, MIRNA, MORNA.

Most Popular "N" Name.... **NICOLE**

☐ **NADA** *(Slavic, 'Hope")*. NADIA, NADINE.

☐ **NADINE** See NADA.

☐ **NAIDA** *(Latin, "River nymph")*.

☐ **NANCY** See ANNE.

☐ **NANETTE** See ANNE.

☐ **NAOMI** *(Hebrew, "Pleasant one")*. The Biblical mother-in-law of Ruth. See NOAMI.

☐ **NARA** *(Old Norse, "Nearest")*. NARINE.

☐ **NATA** *(Hindu, "A dancer")*.

☐ **NATALIE** *(Latin, "Birth day," "Christmas")*. In most countries it has come to mean the Lord's birth day/ In France the name has been shortened to Noelle. NATALA, NATALINA, **NATALINE**, NATHALIA, NATTIE, NETTIE, NOEL, NOELLA French: **NATALIE, NOELLE**; Spanish: **NATALIA**; Russian: **NATASHA**.

☐ **NATASHA** See NATALIE.

☐ **NELL, NELLIE** See ELEANOR.

☐ **NERINE** *(Greek, "A swimmer")*. NERICE, NERISSA, NERITA.

☐ **NERISSA** See NERINE.

☐ **NESSIE** See AGNES.

☐ **NICOLE** *(Greek, Fem. of Nicholas, "Victorious people")*. COLIE, NICAELA, NICOL, NIKKI French: COLLETTE, NICOLETTE; Italian: NICOLA; Greek: NICOLINA.

☐ **NINA** *(Spanish, "Little girl")*. NINETTA French: NINETTE.

☐ **NISSA** *(Scandinavian, "An elf")*.

☐ **NITA** See ANN, JUANITA.

☐ **NIXIE** *(Old German, "Water sprite")*. A legendary mermaid. See BERENICE, VERONICA.

☐ **NOELLE** See NATALIE.

☐ **NORA** NORAH, NORINA, NORITA (See ELEANOR, HONORA).

☐ **NORMA** *(Latin, "A model," "Pattern")*. NOREEN, NORINE.

O

Most Popular
"O" Name...
OLIVIA

☐ **ODESSA** *(Greek, "Of the Odyssey")*.

☐ **OLGA** *(Old Norse, "Peace)*. A popular name in the family of the Russian Czars. ELGA, HELGA, OLIA, OLVA (See OLIVE).

☐ **OLIVE** *(Latin, "Olive tree")*. The olive branch was the emblem of peace. LIVIA, LIVY, NOLA, NOLLIE, OLIVETTE, OLIVIA, OLVA, OLGA Italian: OLIVIA; Russian: OLINKA.

☐ **OLIVIA** See OLIVE.

☐ **OPAL** *(Hindu, "Precious stone")*.

☐ **OPHELIA** *(Greek, "Serpent")*. The symbol of wisdom and invincibility in ancient times.

☐ **ORELA** *(Latin, "one who listens")*.

☐ **ORIANA** See AURELIA.

☐ **OSSIA** *(Gaelic, Fem. of Osbert, "Godlike splendor")*.

P

Most Popular
"P" Name....
PATRICIA

☐ **PAGE** *(Greek, "Child")*. PAIGE.

☐ **PAMELA** *(Greek, "Entirely of honey")*. PAM, PAMELINA, PAMELLA, PAMIE, PAMMY.

☐ **PATIENCE** *(Latin, "Patience")*. One of the Puritan "virtue" names.

☐ **PAT** See PATRICIA.

☐ **PATRICIA.** *(Latin, "Of nobility")*. From the patrician families of Rome/ St. Patrick, the patron saint of Ireland, popularized the name for girls as well as boys.
PAT, PATSY, PATTI, PATTY, TRICIA, TRISH, TRIXIE French: PATRICE; Italian: PATEIZIA.

☐ **PATSY** See PATRICIA.

☐ **PAULA** *(Latin, Paulus, "Little")*. Paulette was the sister of Napoleon/ St. Paula was a 3rd Century saint.
PAULITA, PAULY, POLLY French: PAULETTE, PAULINE; Spanish/Italian: PAOLA, PAOLETTA, PAOLINA; Russian: PAVLA.

☐ **PEARL** *(Latin, "Pearl")*.
PEARLA, PEARLE, PEARLINE (See PERRY).

☐ **PEG/PEGGIE/PEGGY** See MARGARET.

☐ **PENNY** See PENELOPE.

☐ **PETULA** *(Latin, "Searcher")*.

☐ **PHILANA** *(Greek, Fem. of Philander, "Lover of men")*.
PHILENE, PHILINA, PHILLIDA.

☐ **PHILANTHA** *(Greek, "Lover of flowers")*.

☐ **PHOEBE** *(Greek, "The bright")*. PHEBE.

☐ **PHYLLIS** *(Greek, "Green branch")*. The Greek mythological princess who was turned into an almond tree.
PHILLIS, PHIL, PHYLIDA, PHYLIS.

☐ **POLLY** See MARY.
MOLLY, PAULA.

☐ **PRISCILLA** *(Latin, "From the former times")*.
PRIS, PRISSIE.

☐ **PRUDENCE** *(Latin, "Discretion")*. One of the Puritan "virtue" names.
PRU, PRUDY.

Q Most Popular "Q" Name...
QUINTINA

☐ **QUEENA** *(Old English "Queen")*.
QUEENIE.

☐ **QUINTINA** *(Latin, Fem. of Quentin, "The fifth child")*.
QUINTA.

☐ **QUERIDA** *(Spanish, "Darling")*.

Most Popular
"R" Name.......
REBECCA

☐ **RACHEL** *(Hebrew, "Little lamb")*. The Biblical wife of Jacob and mother of Benjamin and Joseph/ The symbol of suffering love and patience.
RAE, RAY, SHELLEY, SHELLY French: **RACHELLE**; Italian: **RACHELE**; Spanish: **RAQUEL**; German: **RAHEL**.

☐ **RAMONA** *(Spanish, "Wise protector")*.
RAMONDA, RAMUNDA.

☐ **RANI** *(Hindu, "Royal")*.
RANA, RAINA, RANEE, RANIA.

☐ **RAQUEL** See **RACHEL**.

✗ ☐ **REBECCA** *(Hebrew, "To bind," "Yoke")*. The Biblical wife of Isaac and mother of Jacob and Esau.
BECKIE, BECKY, REBA, REEBA, REBEKAH, RIVA, RIVKAH Spanish: **REBECA**; German: **REBEKKE**.

☐ **REGINA** *(Latin, "Queen")*.
GINA, REGAN, REGGIE, REYNA, RINA French: **REINE, REINETTE**; Italian/Spanish: **REINA**.

☐ **RENA** *(Hebrew, "Song")*.

☐ **RENATA** *(Latin, "Born again")*.
RENNIE French: **RENEE**.

☐ **RENEE** See **RENATA**.

☐ **RHEA** *(Greek, "A stream")*. In Greek mythology Rhea was the mother of all gods.
REA.

☐ **RHETA** *(Greek, "Speech maker")*.

☐ **RHODA** *(Greek, "Roses, A person from Rhodes")*. See **ROSE**.

☐ **RHONA** See **RONA**.

☐ **RHODIA** See **ROSE**.

☐ **RICA** See **FREDERICA**.

☐ **RICKI, RICKIE** See **FREDERICA**.

☐ **RINA** *(Hebrew, "Ringing")*.

☐ **RITA** See **MARGARET**.

☐ **ROBERTA** *(Old English, Fem. of Robert, "Shining fame")*.
BERT, BERTIE, BOBBETTE, BOBBIE, BOBBY, ROBBIE, ROBBY, ROBIA, ROBIN, ROBINA, ROBINETT, ROBINETTE, ROBINIA French: **ROBINE**; German: **RUPERTA**.

128

☐ **ROBIN** *(Old English, "Robin").*
See ROBERTA.

☐ **ROCHELLE** *(French, "The little rock").*
ROCHELLA, ROCHETTE, SHELL, SHELLY.

☐ **ROLANDA** *(Old German, Fem. of Roland, "The famous land").*
French: ROLANDE; Italian: ORLANDA.

☐ **RONA** *(Scotch, "One of the Hebrides Islands of Scotland").*
RHONA *(See* RONALDA).

☐ **RONALDA** *(Old German, Fem. of Ronald, "Mighty power").*
RON, RHONA, RONA.

☐ **RONNIE** See ROWENA, VERONICA.

☐ **ROSALIE** See ROSE.

☐ **ROSALIND** See ROSALINDA.

☐ **ROSALINDA** *(Spanish, "Pretty rose").*
ROSALIN, ROSALIND, ROSALINDE, ROSALINE, ROSALYN, ROSLYN, ROZ.

☐ **ROSALINE** See ROSALIND.

☐ **ROSANNA** *(English, Combination of Rose and Anna, "Rose of grace").*
ROSANA, ROSANNE.

☐ **ROSE** *(Greek, Rhodos, "A rose").* Two saints were named Rose/ Because of the beauty of this flower, many languages have adopted versions of this name.
RHODIA, ROSALIA, ROSELLA, ROSELLE, ROSIE, ROSINA, ROSINE, ROSY, ROZ, ROZY French: ROSETTE, ROSINE; Italian: ROSALIA, ROSETTA, ROSINA; Spanish: ROSITA; Italian/Spanish/Swedish/Dutch: ROSA; German: ROSALIE; Swiss: ROSEL, ROSI; Irish: ROSALEEN; Greek: RHODA.

☐ **ROSEMARY** *(Latin, The herb "rosemary"/ Latin/Hebrew, "Rose of Mary").*
ROSEMARIE, MARYROSE.

☐ **ROSETTE** See ROSE.

☐ **ROWENA** *(Welsh, "White-haired").* A princess of British legend.
RONNIE, RONNY.

☐ **ROXANNE** *(Persian, "Bright dawn").* Roxana was the wife of Alexander the Great.
ROXANNA, ROXENE, ROXIE, ROXY French: ROXANE.

☐ **ROZ** See ROSALINDA, ROSE.

☐ **RUBY** *(Latin, "Red", "The ruby").*
RUBIA, RUBINA, RUBETTE.

☐ **RUE** *(Greek, "Grief").*

□ **RULA** *(Latin, "A ruler")*.

□ **RUTH** *(Hebrew, "Compassionate")*.
RUTHIA, RUTHIE.

S Most Popular "S" Name....
SARAH

□ **SABINA** *(Latin, "Of the Sabines")*. The Sabines were an ancient Italian people/ Three saints bore the name Sabina.
SAVINA, SAVINE French/German: SABINE.

□ **SABRINA** *(Latin, "From the border")*. The English river Severn was named after the legendary princess Sabrina.
ZABRINA.

□ **SADIE** See SARAH.

□ **SADIRA** *(Arabic, "Constellation")*.

□ **SALINA** *(Latin, "Salty")*.
SALENA.

□ **SALLY** See SARAH.

□ **SALOME** *(Hebrew, Fem. of Solomon, "Peace")*. The daughter of Herodias who demanded the head of John the Baptist.
SALOMA French: SALOMEE; Arabic: SELIMAH, SULEIMA.

□ **SAMANTHA** *(Aramic, "The listener")*.
SAMANTHY, SAMMY.

□ **SAMARA** *(Hebrew, "Guarded by God")*. Biblical city that was the home of the Good Samaritan.
SAMMY.

□ **SANDRA** See ALEXANDRA.

□ **SARAH** (Hebrew, "Princess"). The wife of Abraham and mother of Isaac, was the first named Sarai, "the quarrelsome"; later it was changed by Jehovah.
SADELLA, SADIE, SADYE, SAL, SALLIE, SALLY, SARA, SARENE, SARETTE, SARI, SARINE, SARITA, ZADEE, ZARA, ZARAH Hungarian: SHARI.

□ **SASHA** See ALEXANDRA.

□ **SCARLETT** *(Middle English, "Scarlet colored")*. The heroine of *Gone With the Wind*.

□ **SELDA** See GRISELDA.

□ **SELENA** *(Greek, "The moon")*. Selene was the Greek goddess of the moon.
CELINA, CELINDA, CELINDE, CELINE, SELINA.

□ **SELMA** See ANSELMA.

□ **SEMIRA** *(Hebrew, "The high heavens")*.

130

☐ **SERENA** *(Latin, "Serene one").* Two saints were named Serena/ The Puritans used it as a "virtue" name. SERENITY.

☐ **SHAINA** *(Hebrew, "Beautiful").* SHANA.

☐ **SHANNON** *(Irish, "Slow waters").* The river Shannon in Ireland. CHANNA, CHANNON, SHANE, SHAWNA.

☐ **SHARI** See SARA, SHARON.

☐ **SHARLEEN** See CAROL.

☐ **SHARON** *(Hebrew, A plain in western Israel).* The Song of Solomon sings of the Rose of Sharon. SHARA, SHARI, SHARONA, SHERRI, SHERRY.

☐ **SHEENA** See JANE.

☐ **SHEILA** SHEILAH, SHELLEY, SHELLY (See CECILIA).

☐ **SHELAH** *(Hebrew, "The requested").*

☐ **SHELBY** *(Old English, "From the hillside estate").* SHELLY.

☐ **SHELLEY** *(Old English, "Shell island").* See RACHEL, ROCHELLE, SHEILA, SHELBY.

SHER See CHER.

☐ **SHEREE** See SHERRY, CAROL/ CHARLOTTE.

☐ **SHEREEN** *(Hebrew, "The sweet").*

☐ **SHERRY** See CHER, CAROL/ CHARLOTTE.

☐ **SHERYL** See SHIRLEY, CAROL/ CHARLOTTE.

☐ **SHIRLEY** *(Old English, "Shining meadow").* SHERYL, SHIRL, SHIRLEE, SHIRLEEN, SHIRLENE.

☐ **SIBYL** *(Greek, "A prophetess").* The Sibyls were prophetesses of ancient Greece. CYBIL, SEBILA, SIB, SIBBIE, SIBELLA, SIBIL, SYBIL French: SIBELLE; Italian: SIBILA; Spanish: SEVILLA; German: SIBYLLE.

☐ **SIDRA** *(Latin, "Belonging ⁺o the stars").* SEDRA.

☐ **SIGNA** *(Latin, "Signal," "Sign").* SIGNE Italian: ISGNALE.

☐ **SIGRID** *(Old Norse, "Ruling counsellor").*

☐ **SILVIA** See SYLVIA.

☐ **SIMONE** *(Hebrew, Fem. of Simon, "One who hears").* SIMONA, SIMONETTE.

☐ **SIRENA** *(Greek, "Sweet singer")*. From the Greek mythological sirens.

☐ **SONDRA** See ALEXANDRA.

☐ **SONIA/SONJA/SONYA** See SOPHIA.

☐ **SOPHIA** *(Greek, "Wisdom")*. A name borne by a Byzantine empress, a Christian saint, and a queen of Saxony.
SONIA, SONJA, SOPHRONIA, SOPHY French: SOPHIE; Italian: SOFIA; Scandinavian: SONJA; Polish: ZOFIA; Russian: SONYA.

☐ **STACY** See ANASTASIA.

☐ **STEFFIE** See STEPHANIE.

☐ **STELLA** See ESTELLE.

☐ **STEPHANIE** *(Greek, Fem. of Stephen, "Crowned one")*. St. Stephana was a 16th century saint.
STEFANIA, STEFANIE, STEFFIE, STEPHA, STEPHANA, STEPHANIA, STEVANA, STEVENA French: STEPHANIE; German: STEPHANINE.

☐ **SUSAN** *(Hebrew, "A lily")*. The aprocryphal Susannah, wrongly accused of adultery, was saved by Daniel. Three saints bore the name Susanna.
SUE, SUKE, SUKEY, SUKI, SUKIE, SUSANNA, SUSANNE, SUSETTE, SUSIE, SUZETTA, SUZIE, SUZY, ZUZU French: SUSETTA, SUZANNE, SUZETTE; Spanish: SUSANA; German: SUSCHEN, SUSE; Swiss: ZUZI; Hungarian: ZSA ZSA; Hebrew: SOSHANNAH, SUSANNAH.

☐ **SYBIL** See SIBYL.

☐ **SYLVIA** *(Latin, "Girl of the forest")*.
SILVA, SILVANA, SILVIA, SILVIE.

T Most Popular "T" Name....
TIFFANY

☐ **TABITHA** *(Aramaic, "A gazelle")*.
TAB, TABBY.

☐ **TAFFY** *(Gaelic, "Loved one")*.

☐ **TALIA** *(Greek, "Blooming")*. The Muse of comedy and poetry in Greek myth.

☐ **TAMARA** *(Hebrew, "A palm tree")*. The biblical daughter of David.
TAMAR, TAMMY.

☐ **TANYA** *(Russian, "Friend")*. Short for Tatania.
TANIA (See TITANIA).

☐ **TARA** *(Irish, "Rocky crag")*.

☐ **TEDRA** See THEODORA.

☐ **TEMPERANCE** *(Latin, "Moderation")*. A Puritan "virtue" name.

☐ **TERESA** See THERESA.

☐ **TERRY** See THERESA.

☐ **TESSA** *(Greek, "Fourth born")*. TESS, TESSIE (See THERESA).

☐ **THALIA** *(Greek, "Luxuriant")*. See TALIA.

☐ **THEA** *(Greek, "Goddess")*. See ALTHEA, DOROTHEA.

☐ **THEDA** See THEODORA.

☐ **THELMA** *(Greek, "Nursling")*.

☐ **THEODORA** *(Greek, Fem. of Theodore, "Gift of God")*.
DORA, DOSIA, TEDDI, TEDDIE, TEDDY, TEDRA, THEDA Italian/Spanish: TEODORA; Slavic: FEDORA, FEODORA.

☐ **THEOLA** *(Greek, "Of Godly speech")*.

☐ **THERA** *(Greek, "Untamed")*.

☐ **THERESA** *(Latin, "Reaper")*. St. Theresa was a famous 16th century Spanish nun.
TERESE, TERESITA, TERESSA, TERRI, TERRIE, TERRY, TESS, TESSA, TESSIE, TESSY, TRACEY, TRACIE, TRACY French: THERESE; Italian: TERESA, TERESINA; German: THERESIA, TRESA; Hungarian: TEREZIA.

☐ **THIRLA** *(Hebrew, "Delight")*. In the Song of Solomon: "Thou art beautiful ... as Tirzah."
TIRZAH.

☐ **THYRA** *(Old Norse, "Child of war")*. Tyr was the Scandinavian god of war/ Tuesday is a "Tyr's day."

☐ **TIFFANY** *(Greek, "Appearance of God")*.
TIFFIE, TIFFY.

☐ **TINA** Short for names ending in "tina," "tine."
See ALBERTINA, BETTINA, CHRISTINE, etc.

☐ **TOBY** *(Hebrew, "God is good")*. TOBE, TOBEY, TOVA, TOVE, TYBLE.

☐ **TONIA** See ANTOINETTE.

☐ **TONI** See ANTOINETTE.

☐ **TRACY** See TERESA.

☐ **TRICIA** See PATRICIA.

☐ **TRINA** See CATHERINE.

☐ **TRIXIE** See BEATRICE.

☐ **TRUDY** *(Old German, "Loved one")*.

☐ **TUESDAY** *(Old English, "Born on Tuesday")*.

133

Most Popular
"U" Name....
URSULA

☐ **UDA** *(Old German, "Prosperous")*. UDELLE.

☐ **ULRICA** *(Old German, Fem. of Ulric, "All ruler")*.

☐ **UNA** *(Latin, "The one")*. ONA, ONNIE, UNITY Irish: OONA.

☐ **URSULA** *(Latin, "Little she bear")*. ORSA, URSA, URSULINE French: URSULE; Italian: ORSOLA; Spanish: URSOLA.

Most Popular
"V" Name....
VALERIE

☐ **VAL** Short for names beginning with "Val."

☐ **VALA** *(Old German, "The chosen one")*.

☐ **VALDA** *(Old Norse, "Destructive in battle")*. VELDA.

☐ **VALENTINA** *(Latin, Fem. of Valentine, "Strong")*. St. Valentine is the 3rd Century saint whose day we celebrate each February 14. VALIVALEDA, VALENCIA, VALENTIA, VALENTINE (See **VALERIE**).

☐ **VALERIE** *(Latin, "Strong")*. Valerie is the French version of the name Valeria, which has the same root as Valentina. VAL, VALAREE, VALE, VALERY, VALLY, VALORA, VALOREE, VALORY Italian: VALERIA.

☐ **VALESKA** *(Slavic, Fem. of Vladislav, "Ruling glory")*.

☐ **VALONIA** *(Latin, "From the valley")*.

☐ **VANESSA** *(Greek, "A butterfly")*. VAN, VANNA, VANNY Italian: VANNA; Greek: PHANESSA.

☐ **VANORA** *(Welsh, "White wave")*.

☐ **VARINA** *(Slavic, "Stranger")*. See BARBARA.

☐ **VASHTI** *(Persian, "Beautiful")*.

☐ **VEDA** *(Hindu, "Sacred knowledge")*.

☐ **VELMA** See WILHELMINA.

☐ **VERA** *(Latin, "Truth")*. VERENE, VERITY, VERLA (See VERONICA).

134

☐ **VERENA** *(Old German, "Sacred wisdom").*

☐ **VERNA** *(Latin, "Springtime").* VERNE, VERNETTE, VERNICE, VERNITA, VIRENA.

☐ **VERONICA** *(Latin, "True image").* St. Veronica gave Jesus a cloth to wipe his face, leaving his image imprinted on it. RONNIE, RONNY, VERA, VERONIKA, VONNIE, VONNY.

☐ **VICTORIA** *(Latin, "Victory").* Both Spain and England have had Queens named Victoria. VICKI, VICKIE, VICKY French: VICTOIRE; Italian: VITTORIA; Spanish: VITORIA.

☐ **VINA** *(Spanish, "From the vinyard").*

☐ **VIOLET** *(Latin, "The violet").* IOLANTHE, TOLETTA, VI, VIOLA, VIOLE, VIOLETA, VIOLETTA, YOLANDA, YOLANTHE French: VIOLETTE, YOLANDE, YOLETTE; Spanish: VIOLANTE.

☐ **VIRGINIA** *(Latin, "A virgin").* The state of Virginia was named by Sir Walter Raleigh in honor of Elizabeth the Virgin Queen of England. GINGER, GINNIE, GINNY, VERGIE, VIRGIE French: VIRGINIE.

☐ **VIVIAN** *(Latin, Viva, "Full of life").* Both feminine and masculine. VIV, VIVA, VIVIA, VIVIANA, VIVIE, VIVIENNE, VIVYAN German: VITAIIANA.

☐ **VONNIE** See VERONICA.

W Most Popular "W" Name . . . **WENDY**

☐ **WANDA** *(Old German, "Wanderer").*

☐ **WANNETTA** *(Old English, "Pale").*

☐ **WELDA** See WALDA.

☐ **WENDY** See GWENDOLYN.

☐ **WHITNEY** *(Old English, "The white island").*

☐ **WILDA** *(Old German, "Untamed").* WYLDA.

☐ **WILHELMINA** *(Old German, Fem. of William, "Resolute guardian").* Wilhelmina was Queen of Holland. BILLIE, BILLY, HELMA, MINNIE, MINNY, VILMA, WILHELMA, WILLA, WILLAMENA, WILLANN, WILLETTA, WILLETTE, WILMA, WILMENA, VELMA French: GUILLELMINE, GUILLEMETTE, GUILLETTE, MIMI; Italian:

GUGLIELMA; Spanish: GUILLEL-MINA, GUILLEMMA; Dutch: WILLE-MYN; German: HELMINE, MINA, MINCHEN, MINNA; Swedish: VIL-HELMINE.

☐ **WILMA** See WILHELMINA.

☐ **WILONA** (Old English, "Object of desire").

☐ **WIN** See WINIFRED, EDWINA.

☐ **WINIFRED** (Old German, "Peaceful field"). Winifred was a 17th Century saint.
FREDDY, WIN, WINNIE, WINNY.

☐ **WINONA** (American Indian, "First born daughter").

☐ **WYLDA** See WILDA.

☐ **WYNNE** (Welsh, "White").
WINNIE, WYNETTA, WYNETTE.

X Most Popular
"X" Name....
XENA

☐ **XAVIERA** (Arabic, Fem. of Xavier, "Brilliant").

☐ **XENA** (Greek, "The guest").
XENIA, ZENIA.

☐ **XENIA** (Greek, "Hospitable").
ZENA, ZENIA.

Y Most Popular
"Y" Name....
YVONNE

☐ **YOLANDA** See VIOLET.

☐ **YVETTE** See YVONNE.

☐ **YVONNE** (Old French, Fem. of Yves, "Archer").
EVONNE, YVETTE.

Z Most Popular
"Z" Name....
ZELDA

☐ **ZABRINA** See SABRINA.
☐ **ZARA** See SARAH.
☐ **ZEA** (Latin, "A grain").
☐ **ZELDA** See GRISELDA.
☐ **ZELLA** (Greek, "Zeal").
☐ **ZELMA** See ANSELMA.
☐ **ZENA** (Persian, "Woman"). See XENIA.
☐ **ZENIA** See XENIA.
☐ **ZERA** (Hebrew, "Seedling").
ZERAH.
☐ **ZIA** (Latin, "A grain").
ZEA.
☐ **ZOE** (Greek, "Life"). A name used in Egypt to translate the Biblical name Eve.